MW00891574

Events Dictate

Life, Love & Leadership

The Collected Essays of
SY OGULNICK

Edited by Steve A. Zuckerman

Special thanks to Laurie Bennett for her efforts and contributions in bringing this project to press.

Dedication

When I first met Lenette, I was born anew. In the sixty-nine years we've been together, nothing has changed. I owe her me. I also owe much to my many years of working with staff, children, professionals, and entrepreneurs. They have all taught me so much about love, life, and leadership.

CONTENTS

Foreword ix
From the Editor xi

AUTOBIOGRAPHICAL ESSAYS 1
Aspiring to be an Effective Leader 3
The Storm 4
Okinawa 6
The Return Home 9
A Journey Of Discovery 11
The Birth Of My Philosophy 13
Was It Now... Or Forever? 14
"Serendipity" The Story Of Camp Shasta 16
Turning Point 20
The Encounter 21
Lenette's Vision 22
Closing of Camp Letter 23
Las Vegas 25
The Olmec Heads 26
On Our Way Home 31
Back To Big Changes 32
The 9th Symphony 33
My Memory Bank 34
Haiku Thoughts 35

ON RELATIONSHIPS 39
The Challenges Facing Human Relationships 41
Belief vs. Fact 42
Too Many Questions, Too Few Answers 43
Times Like Today 45
Being Open 46
Two To Tango 47
Consequences 49
The Challenges of Communication 50
Speaking The Truth 51
Being Creative With Relationships 52
Power In Relationships 54
Is Being Yourself Ever Really Being Just You? 55
Power And Influence 56
Why Dialogue Is Important To Me 57
Genuine Communication Is Never Easy 58

ON SELF **59**

Our Journey To Self-Actualization 61
Society vs. The Individual 63
Changing Times 65
We Each Are Who We Are 66
Events Are Experiences 67
Candid: Is There A Better Way To Be? 68
A Desire To Grow 69
Are You A Leader? 71
Bureaucracy And System 73
Making Differences Work 75
We Are Products Of Our Past 76
Creating The Environment For Change 77
Becoming Oneself 78
Being Present 79
Creating Your "Better Self" 80
Can People Become More Than Who They Were? 81
The People In Our Lives 82

ON LEADERSHIP AND POWER **83**

Leadership Basics 85
The Best Kind Of Leadership 88
Events Dictate 89
A Leader's Words And Behavior 90
Who Invites Change? 92
Enlightened Leadership—Where Art Thou? 93
Quality Leadership 95
Dogs That Hunt And Dogs That Don't 97
The True Entrepreneur 98
Working With Volunteers 100
More On Power 102
Leadership And Role Model Workshops 103
Workshop—Terms And Conditions 104
An Experiment In Being Present 105
Power, Failure And Knowing Oneself 107
Listening And Understanding 109
Confirmation 110
Moving Towards Openness 112
Leadership—By Accident Or Design? 114
Designated Leaders 115
It's Not About Tools 116
The Damage A Bad Leader Does 117

Defining Leadership 118
The Inner Circle 119
Power And The Inner Circle 120
The Root Of Failure 121
Being A Leader 122
What Makes A Good Leader? 123
Populism Is Not Leadership 124

ON PHILOSOPHY AND TEACHING 125
My Philosophy 127
Bernard Palissy 129
The Origins Of My Philosophy 131
The "Problem Child" 133
The Classroom Environment 135
The Space Between 136
Teachers As Leaders 137
Philosophy At Work 138
Parents As Leaders 139
Ideal Role Models 140
Being Is Not An Act 141
What Can We Learn From Lecture? 142
Training Potential Leaders 143
Socrates, Aristotle, And Plato 144

ON GENUINE DIALOGUE 145
Rules Of Engagement 147
Technology vs. Genuine Dialogue 149
Communication Is The Problem 151
Dialogue 153
Free Speech, Facts And Opinion 154
Fact, Fiction, Opinion, And Expectation 155
Emotional vs. Rational Thought 157
Like Family 158

ANIMAL STORIES 159
Our Beloved Animals 161
Lizzy 162
Call Of The Wild 164
Heidi, Brutus, And Cleo 167

ON AGING—A PERSONAL JOURNEY 169
On Aging—My View 171

Live And Love Now 173
What's Important 174
Changes 175
Our Move 177
Settling In 179
Our New Reality 181
We Are Learning 182
94th Birthday 183
The Benefits Of Community 185
More Thoughts On Aging 187
Diminishing Choices 188
Pure Love 189
More On Aging 190
Another Way Of Looking At Aging 191
What Visiting Means To Us 192
Time Flies 193
Aging Differently? 194
How I'm Aging 195
Old Friends 196
Aging—A New Mindset 197
Communicating With The Aging 198
Aging—Not For the Weak 199
A Now Thing 200
A Blessing? 201

OTHER THOUGHTS **203**

It's Simple 205
Truth 206
Focusing On The Future 208
Our Changing Planet 209
Thoughts On A World Government 210
Where Are We Headed? 211
Who Will Lead? 212
A Sad State Of Affairs 215
Guns 217
The Times We Live In 218
Selecting Leaders 219

Foreword

I first met Sy Ogulnick in 1965 at the end of my freshman year at UCLA. He'd posted an advertisement for camp counselors on a bulletin board in the student employment center, and I needed a summer job. Sy came to campus to interview me. I was surprised by this short man of powerful stature with a diagonal scar across his forehead and nose because he had a voice that was soft and calm and eyes that showed sensitivity, depth, and caring. I felt that I was in the presence of an amazing individual, which was corroborated later when I learned that, as a youth, he had been a tough brawler on the streets of Chicago. Now, before me, was a man dedicated to the mission of helping kids. He did this at his beloved Camp Shasta, a forest retreat owned and operated by him and his wife Lenette, where he gave kids an opportunity to learn about nature and develop self-reliance in a community of their peers.

Sy hired me for that summer, during which time I learned that his philosophy of life was an accepting one in that he saw the best in every person he met and knew how to help them access and express it. I personally experienced this from the moment I arrived at camp when he entrusted me with duties I hadn't known I could fulfill. He handed me a book called *The Web of Life* and told me, "You're going to be our nature specialist and teach the kids about ecology." Thus, a decade before I became a college professor, he intuited an ability I didn't know I had.

During my life-changing ten weeks that summer as a counselor at Camp Shasta, I witnessed Sy listen to and thoughtfully consider the ideas, perspectives, and feelings of everyone, regardless of their position in the camp's social hierarchy. He gave us all a life-long lesson in leadership when he showed us how to get along with each other and work effectively together in groups. He also modeled how a good leader is able to truly listen to others and appreciate the value of their beliefs and feelings.

The stories and essays in this book relate a hard-won philosophy of life based on the importance of honoring the life struggles people have endured and making them aware of their capacity for personal growth and positive change. Sy Ogulnick shows us the importance of living each day with an openness to learning from what life brings us. It is through such acceptance that we can become the persons we were meant to be.

This book will allow you to experience Sy's grit, unfailing positivity, incisive creative mind, and his heartfelt faith in people's capacity to learn, grow, and evolve.

George J. Lough II, Ph.D.
October 30th 2022

From the Editor

For as long as I've known Sy, he has generously shared his unique take on leadership, relationships, power, and, more recently, his views on aging. In compiling this collection of his many essays, I've attempted to make as few changes as possible to preserve Sy's voice and intent. The essays are grouped first by overall topic and then ordered to maximize context and continuity. Some stories and viewpoints reappear occasionally, but they remain to conserve Sy's vision.

I sincerely hope everyone finds a measure of inspiration and perhaps a bit of their own history in Sy's stories and words of wisdom. I believe that even those who have had the privilege of knowing and working with Sy will gain new insight into his larger-than-life persona and thought-provoking philosophies.

Steve A. Zuckerman
October 20th 2022

AUTOBIOGRAPHICAL ESSAYS

Aspiring To Be An Effective Leader

14 October 2020

After I retired from working with leaders and their key personnel, I sought an outlet to express what I know is essential if one aspires to be an effective leader. Writing seemed the best vehicle to continue teaching the solutions to relationship and leadership issues. Short essays have become my way of sharing my thoughts. When inspiration strikes, I add a few Haiku, always taken from the meat of the paper.

Working with leaders, organizations, and families of many leaders, I witnessed significant changes in people's behavior and attitude. Dialogue happened more frequently, as did listening and understanding. Going forward, I will reflect on this and my teaching and classroom days with fifth and sixth graders and, of course, camp. I clearly remember all these experiences and their impact on how people related to each other. To this day, I am told how meaningful they were—music to my mind and heart.

The work we did in the workplace, the work counselors did at camp, and how I related to my students in the classroom made a difference in the lives of most that participated. This way of connecting and communicating is what I will share in other essays. No theories or "hare-brained" ideas, just the facts. I will also share my thoughts about the destruction the sicknesses of discrimination and hatred have wrought on societies for many centuries.

Writing my outlet
Speaking used to be my style
I found another way

The Storm
15 July 2021

Experience does not force learning upon us. Yet every event and experience has the potential to teach us if we are receptive. Still, the outcomes are never guaranteed, even in the best of well-planned events. I stress that the more present we are, the more each event is potentially loaded with meaningful lessons. If we are not fully present in the moments of an experience, we may miss its benefits. Allow me to share a profound experience and what I learned about myself.

In September 1945, I was on an LST in the middle of the Pacific heading for Okinawa. An LST is a small vessel that displaces only about 10 feet of water and is built to land on shore with tanks and trucks. As fortune would have it, we were heading directly into a large typhoon. Because of the storm's size and the type of ship we were on, the only course of action was to head directly into the storm.

The ship was loaded top to bottom, and everything was tied down, including all hatches leading to the deck. As we drew closer to the storm, the captain announced over the "bitch box" that prayer services were being conducted in the mess hall and directed all crew into the bowels of the ship. I decided to witness the typhoon; if we went under, I would witness that too.

The space between the hatch and the deck was roped. The hatch was locked, so there was no getting out on the deck. Still, I could stand between the rope and the hatch. Through the hatch window, I saw everything as it took place. It was one of the most extraordinary experiences in my life.

Cigar-shaped clouds began to rush towards me; waves grew until they were above my head. I was looking at nothing but water and then watching it disappear as we were lifted to the top of a mountain of ocean.

We were a cork, riding on the crest of each wave or bobbing in its valley. I am sure I fell asleep for brief periods, overwhelmed by the experience, but I witnessed the power of nature beyond anything before and since. As the storm grew in intensity, I felt no fear of death. Instead, I felt a certain strength I do not remember having before this event—a sense that I would be able to handle whatever life threw at me.

Okinawa
14 September 2019

Humans need each other. To begin with, we could not exist without others bringing us into this world. Of course, we understand this and why our parents are so vital to us. As we grow, so does our need for others. I have shared the story below many times because it strongly emphasizes that our need for each other as humans never goes away. And, when we meet and serve each other's needs, our regard for each other becomes more important.

Over the years, I've been asked to write about the three POWs and our relationship on Okinawa. To this day, I feel the influence they had on my growth because of our working together. Their faces remain etched in my mind and heart. Even now, as I write this, it brings a smile and a warm feeling. They helped make me the person I became.

My respect and regard for them began on day one, and I felt this in return. None of it was planned, which is why I call it a "happening." On Okinawa, the war was over, but many Japanese soldiers remained alive and well while living in elaborate caves. The potential for danger was a problem that had to be resolved, and while doing so, I met three Japanese soldiers who became my "best friends."

I was part of a squad that drove into the hills near Naha, the largest city in Okinawa. We had two prisoners with us who we would send into caves to convince anyone inside that the war was over and that the best thing they could do was lay down their arms and come out. They would be safe and cared for—proof of which was provided by the two sent into the cave.

If they did not come out, we would proceed to blow up the entrance to the cave. But in this case, three soldiers came out with the two we sent in. From the looks on their faces, it was clear the three thought they would be killed. At that moment, the sergeant yelled out, "Ogulnick! Take the prisoners to the compound."

We had arrived in a ½-ton truck, so it meant he wanted me to drive and take them to the compound. I had never driven anything before, but boy, did I want to. I had no intention of telling the sergeant, "I could not drive." If I faced a typhoon and other life-threatening experiences, I could drive a truck—no problem.

I got into the driver's side and immediately began reading the metal instruction plate on the dash. The three prisoners and guard climbed into the back of the truck. With pure fear and excitement, I got the motor turned on and began heading downhill in one of the many gears. The truck responded in a series of jerks, and the four in the back immediately fell to the floor, holding on for dear life. All this while I began my first-ever experience as a driver of a vehicle!

A week passed, and my sergeant instructed me to build an outdoor warehouse for equipment found in the fields and separate what might be repaired and stored from the stuff they were dumping in the ocean. He added that I pick up a few prisoners to use as laborers to do the heavy lifting.

On my trip to the compound, I saw the same three that came out of the cave and whom I drove, and we immediately smiled at each other. Indeed, we each remembered our close call with death during the drive! I realized then that they were and had to be my coworkers. How could I know we would become close and caring and, yes, best friends?

There was Yamamoto, in his late thirties, and a former bank executive from Hiroshima. Ohara, a tall and muscular man in his late twenties, was a former streetcar conductor in Tokyo. And Kato, a small guy who formally was an actor in Tokyo.

Once together, it took them five minutes to realize I was a nineteen-year-old that knew nothing. They immediately took over and began the process of organizing and constructing our warehouse. I also recognized that they never made light of my role as a leader. Invariably, they would play deaf and dumb so that when officers requested equipment, the three coworkers made sure I appeared to be the power that either gave or denied the request.

Using *Life* magazine, we taught each other our languages. My Japanese and their English became good enough to communicate, laugh a bundle, and get things done. My trust in the three of them was total. I questioned none of their decisions, and whatever equipment was requested—radios, field telephones, etc., was handled smoothly and effectively. They always ensured I got credit for the results we achieved. They taught me leadership. Together, we eventually built the best and largest outdoor warehouse on Okinawa with forklifts, cherry pickers, a crane, and three trucks.

As the warehouse grew, so did our crew. We soon had twelve POWs working in the yard. One day, a POW ran into the hills attempting to join the Japanese soldiers still fighting the war. I grabbed my carbine and headed off to recapture him, but Ohara and Kato tackled me and held me down, explaining that Yamamoto went after the runaway. Immediately, I thought I'd lost two prisoners! Ohara and Kato assured me all would be well and that Yamamoto would return with the runaway. An hour or so later, he did just that. Yamamoto then lined our workers up with me in the front and spoke harshly to the prisoner. After Yamamoto delivered a slap to his face, we all went back to work. This event was never repeated again.

We commit to do
And become one in our goals
We do not fail any

The leader leads us
Because they do the job best
We participate

The Return Home
14 September 2019

The yard grew, and a card file created by Yamamoto was perfect. Each item in the yard had its place and condition noted. We had become a big yard that held all kinds of equipment that would ultimately be shipped back to the States, used locally, or disposed of. The Pacific was our dumping ground.

The day came when the four of us discussed our return home. Ohara, the streetcar conductor, looked forward to returning home. Kato, the actor, also wanted to return. Yamamoto, the senior of the group, had lost his whole family to the Hiroshima bomb and desired to remain on Okinawa. There was nothing for him to return to. I wrote letters on their behalf supporting that their wishes be fulfilled. In my ignorance and youth, I never thought of remaining in touch with them. To this day, I am sorry for that.

My company captain administered my GED exam and offered to arrange for me to go to radar school in the Philippines. That meant a year-plus of schooling and a promotion to 2nd lieutenant upon graduation. At the same time, I was given the opportunity to return home to civilian life. I chose to return to Chicago and my family. Because of my captain's influence, I looked forward to beginning my formal education. Although I had no idea what that would be, the thought of becoming a student excited me.

When the day came for me to leave Okinawa and the military, I met with my three dear friends. It was a painful experience I will always remember, as I will never forget them. Over the fifteen months we had worked together, we had become family, and it was painful to say goodbye. We all hugged and cried at our parting. They had contributed to my becoming a man and, as I was to discover, a leader.

Yamamoto was my primary teacher, but Kato and Ohara also taught me what relationship, respect, and regard meant. We truly and deeply had this for each other. Throughout my entire experience on Okinawa, they became my closest and dearest friends. How blessed I was to have them in my life!

When I reflect on this experience, I see that from the moment I saw these men with their hands over their heads, I felt empathy and sadness for them. They really believed we would kill them when they walked out of that cave. What happened instead was a friendship I hope they carried with them throughout their lives. I certainly have.

We meet and become
Becoming what we know not
And why becoming

I allow you in
Takes courage to allow this
Yet, what other course?

You give me your self
Rare to be given freely
Never take lightly

A Journey Of Discovery

02 November 2021

This is a story about my journey of discovery. Although it began with me thinking I was in charge, events themselves took control and went the way circumstances often dictated. Yes, I was the driver behind the wheel, so one might conclude it was my choice. Perhaps, but I'll let my story answer that question.

After returning from the service, I used the G.I. Bill to enroll in a local pre-med school in Chicago. At that time, pre-med was a three-year college course that preceded more advanced medical studies. I needed some pocket money. Since I preferred being my own boss, I came up with the idea of running my own day camp. I bought a three-seat station wagon and put the word out that I would be taking care of children during the work week. Soon, I had fifteen boys and girls to take care of.

Listening and watching, it soon became apparent that the kids had their own ideas about how they wanted to spend their day together. I quickly established that it was my job to meet their desires, not mine, and I did my best to do so. Giving kids their own voice was one fundamental approach to how I worked with them.

Instead of constructing activities for the day, I opened our morning gathering by asking each what they wanted to do. I made it my responsibility to fulfill their suggestions. The more I did this, the more they expressed themselves. Little did I know their words were training me, nor did they realize the power of their words.

Those actions, as I came to understand, were a philosophy of leadership. Getting followers to express themselves and making it the leader's job to fulfill their wishes, assuming the activity was safe, was good for both the individuals and the group.

A few years later, while a student at UCLA, the need to make a few dollars made itself known again. As good fortune would have it, my brother-in-law found a perfect parcel of land to rent out in

Malibu Canyon, and in little time we had a day camp called Purple Sage.

Soon after we opened, those few children grew into hundreds, necessitating a fleet of 35 small buses and the expansion of our well-trained staff accordingly. The activities at Purple Sage ranged from horses to anything and everything the campers wanted and everything we believed they needed. The philosophy of listening to children and implementing their wishes with small groups proved to be a remarkable success.

The Birth Of My Philosophy

04 October 2020

In 1948, we opened a small day camp in Los Angeles. We were just a few young, enthusiastic adults, so we spent most of our time discussing logistics, not a philosophy to teach and live by. But when the camp exploded far beyond our expectations, we had to employ considerably more people. So, we began developing a practical philosophy for this purpose. Yet, we had no specific goals in mind beyond simply playing games and teaching non-swimmers how to swim.

We held monthly meetings throughout the winter with staff and discussed our responsibilities to each child and the best ways to meet the children's, parents, and our own expectations. My experiences in Chicago with our few children and their participation in selecting activities became our starting point for building a meaningful philosophy.

Our campers ranged in age from kids as young as three to those in their early teens. It is worth emphasizing the participation we asked of them. Besides discussing their activities as a group, they created their own plan for the day. Groups were a maximum of 8 campers, a young adult leader, and a teenage assistant.

No higher-ups made a schedule for their day's activities. If it required scheduling, such as horseback riding, they assigned someone to go to the stable and establish a time for lessons and horses. Also noteworthy is that the group stayed together even if someone feared horses. If one or two chose not to ride, they helped out at the stable while the group went out on the trail.

Dialogue and a deep understanding and respect for each other took place within the group. They walked, talked, learned, and played together every day at camp. They became a tribe where participation was made easy. None were excluded or silent. As the leader and role model, the counselor blended in until events dictated they take charge.

Was It Now... Or Forever?

22 July 2021

The following is an actual experience. What took place could not have happened, and yet it did…

It was a beautiful Sunday in July 1955, and for some strange reason, I decided to drive to our Day Camp, "Purple Sage," in Malibu Canyon and go for a horseback ride. It was a rare desire since I frequently rode a horse around camp when it was in session, checking on activities and the kids. Still, I felt compelled to go to camp and take a Sunday ride.

When I arrived at the corral, I expected "71" to come running to me. 71 was a big Tennessee Walker named for the number branded on her flank. Usually, when I was anywhere near the corral, she would whinny and come over. Yet, for the first time in our 10-year relationship, she did not even look in my direction. Instead, a horse I had never ridden came over and nuzzled me as if to say, "I've been waiting for you. Let's go for a ride."

It was a Strawberry Rhone with a gentle reputation and an easy ride. Strawberry's round back made it easy for me to ride her bareback with only a hackamore around her nose—no bridle or saddle. How much sweeter a ride can there be?

We crossed into one of Bob Hope's large meadows that bordered camp property. Strawberry began a gentle lope when suddenly she began to prance, and the lope became a slow gallop. I gripped the halter as she began a full-out run. And suddenly, it wasn't me, and it wasn't 1950. Out of nowhere, other riders surrounded me with sabers in their hands, charging towards a village I could see in the distance. In that instant, I realized I also held a saber and was a warrior attacking a village on the steppes of Asia. All of this was as clear as any reality I have experienced!

Then, without warning, Strawberry stepped into a gopher hole at full speed, and we both went flying. We both got up from the ground, dirty but unhurt. Strangely, instead of heading back to the corral at a run, Strawberry came to me and knelt, waiting for me to mount. Slowly and in deep thought, we headed back to the corral. As crazy as it seems, I was sure it happened, and I was equally sure the horse felt it too.

When I returned home, Lenette remarked on my dirty clothes, and I shared the event in detail with her. I didn't have a scratch on me, which made me consider how lucky Strawberry and I were. Perhaps we were protected by our mutual momentary mind trip. To this day, it remains a mystery.

I am in the now
Maybe not but possible
Is real always real?

I live the present
But do I live only here?
Maybe not, maybe?

"Serendipity"
The Story Of Camp Shasta
17 July 2022

In 1958 Lenette and I decided we needed to leave Purple Sage, our day camp on a beautiful estate we leased in Malibu Canyon. We sought our own land for both a resident camp and, if close to Los Angeles, continue our very successful day camp.

We began our search in LA and continued to expand it, heading northward in California. We found beautiful land, but with prices that were impossible for us. The journey kept expanding until we reached the small town of Redding, California, where land, we were told, might be in our price range.

As a matter of fact, we had no idea what our "price range" was, being entirely ignorant of what we were doing. This is why I title the tale "Serendipity" because, as you will read, that is what it was. We may have been blind to costs, but not when it came to creating programs for youth.

We searched the country around Redding for a day and found nothing to our liking. As night fell, it grew pitch black, and a driving rain began to fall. On our way back to our motel in Redding, we became lost. I saw a man leaning against a streetlight and went over to ask him for directions. He was standing outside a small bar in the pouring rain—drunk, which, of course, was why he was out in the rain. Surprisingly, this turned out to be an incredible stroke of luck!

Here we were, talking to the drunk outside in the pouring rain. He gave me directions and, as an afterthought, asked, "Why are you here?"

These four words changed our lives. I said we were here looking for land to buy for a kid's camp.

The drunk immediately responded, "Go see Carl. He owns lots of forest land. Head up that road you just passed. His house is the only one on the road."

Since we had already traveled nearly 700 miles looking for a miracle and being there anyway, we drove away from the drunk and went searching for the house he described. So, on a pitch black night, in a rainstorm, and on the words of a drunk, we went seeking without the slightest idea what we would find. Yet, we found the house exactly where he said it would be. I knocked on the door, and a lady greeted us. She heard my story and invited us in to wait for her husband.

About a half-hour later, he returned home. In every respect imaginable, he was a wilderness man with huge hands that swallowed mine as we shook. He heard me out as I explained what we were looking for, and he replied he had 80 acres right up the hill that might work for me.

"Do you ride a horse?" he asked. "We can see the land tomorrow. The road is an ancient dirt road that will be too muddy to drive with this rain."

Lenette and I had obligations with the LA Board of Education, so I asked him if we could meet the following weekend. That following weekend it was still raining, but he had horses saddled and waiting for us, nevertheless. So, away we went across a large meadow, a creek, and through virgin forest to the meadow and woodlands that would eventually become camp.

When I saw the meadow and surrounding forest, I almost cried because I just knew it was OUR land. The seller could tell from my behavior that I wanted to buy the property. Since now that the cat was out of the bag, it appeared I had done myself no favors. I was left to assume the negotiations to follow would be very one-sided.

Before we began talking about money in earnest, I got off the horse to drink from a miracle spring. The crystal-clear water pouring out of rocks tasted like water beyond any water I have ever tasted, and it was not a trickle but a flow. He told me this was ancient water coming through veins deep in the earth from majestic Mt. Shasta, which I could see to the north.

He asked me if I could handle $6000. I almost passed out thinking he meant per month. That was the end of my crazy dreams and hopes.

He saw my face and shoulders hang in sadness and said, "Total!" I reached for his hand, and we shook, and both of us broke into big smiles. "This price will allow me to log the forest this winter," he added.

"Okay," I replied, not knowing anything about logging or the logging world. I would own this magnificent land, which is what drove me at that moment. But before we sealed the deal, I said, "Your freedom to log is only for this coming winter because we will be building out camp so we can open in 1960." Surprisingly, he agreed and put it in the sales agreement.

Consider the following serendipitous event that happened next. It rained well over 100 inches that winter, and because of mud and the difficulty of using machinery, he could not log a twig. Camp Shasta remained untouched. But there's more.

The land was a prime property for logging and an ideal location for a logging camp. After the purchase was published, a logging company in Redding placed an enormous gate and lock at the entrance of our one-mile dirt road into camp. I was locked out of my land. The sign on the gate gave the address in Redding, and that's where I immediately headed.

Getting to Redding and the lumber company's office didn't take long. I went to the front desk, announced my name, and was told the boss would see me. Obviously, they expected someone to visit. I was that someone.

The guy sat behind a big desk and, without hesitation, said, "You don't belong in this country. We'll buy your property for more than you paid for it."

No greeting, no introductions, just his declaration that "I don't belong." With that, he reached into his desk, pulled out a .45, and laid it on the desk.

Again, he said, "You really do not belong up here. You're much better off staying in LA."

I stood up, leaned over the desk, placed my face about 6 inches from his, and said, "Go f — yourself," and walked out of the office.

I drove back to our property, broke off the lock, put a chain around the gatepost, and pulled the gate out of the ground. I dragged the gate to our property line, dug two holes, and installed our new gate. For all I know, it's still there.

But there was more serendipity to come. A major lumber company owned the land that abutted our south property line. The spring and the road touched our property, but they were on their property. Close to us, but theirs. I contacted them to do some "horse trading," and they were wide open to the idea.

Then another two miracles occurred. I proposed to trade 10 acres of virgin forest on our northwest corner, far from what was to become camp, to the big lumber company. They agreed, and in return for the 10 acres, they gave us 15 acres, including the spring and road! And, oh yes, they also purchased the other lumber company in Redding that said "I didn't belong" and wanted our land. Case closed and all in our favor. Serendipity? Of course!

So, Camp Shasta came to be and opened in the summer of 1960. The staff and campers built the cabins for five double bunks. Each group was free to do anything they wanted with their summer homes. And, of course, they did.

Turning Point
24 August 2020

When Lenette and I decided to leave formal education behind, it had nothing to do with success or failure in the system. We loved teaching, and we loved being on our own. We know both very well, but having our independence, even if unpredictable—and with no assurance of income—was still more appealing. Without fear, but with faith in our abilities, we chose our own path and never looked back.

My essays touch upon much of what I have come to realize in my waning years. What helped this take place are the remembrances of children and staff, who are now ages 60 through 80, and the adult professionals and entrepreneurs I've worked with over the past thirty years.

My epiphany that "power is the problem to the answers most leaders seek" is among the most important. When I discovered this as a visiting mentor teaching better staff and leader relationships, I was shocked at my ignorance. I knew how to train staff to optimize their contributions to their work, but I never had any inkling that I, as a leader, was a major contributor to the personal relationship problems within my organization.

Following my awakening, I became a serious student of leadership and power. If I was to teach others how to have a more harmonious workplace, I had to convince leaders they were the problem they had paid me to resolve. Most of them listened and prospered.

However, many leaders around the country hired me expecting I'd give them tools to fix their relationship problems. Of course, tools don't do the job. Only being authentic does. The results are inevitable when leaders are real, meaning they are perceived as authentic by all they interact with. Authenticity empowers staff, and everyone else, to grow and become more themselves for everyone's betterment.

The Encounter

24 October 2022

The 2nd week after we purchased the 80 acres near Montgomery Creek, California, Lenette and I drove 600 miles from L.A. to get a feel of our pristine forest, meadow, and magnificent spring. Our intentions were to explore all of it, touch the huge trees, visit and drink from the miracle spring on our property, and see and get wet in our northern border, Richardson Creek. On all sides, there were beautiful forests where wild animals were the only close residents.

The trip from Los Angeles was an all-day drive, and in 1959, highway 99 was a narrow two-lane road used essentially by farmers. We loved the sights and meandering highway because it was OUR land we were driving to. For us, it was something wonderful and challenging.

After having dinner in Redding, California., we arrived at camp as dusk settled in. We threw our ponchos and sleeping bags down by a large oak tree, beyond what was to become center field in our baseball diamond, and settled in for the night. Heidi, the best watchdog anywhere, slept at our feet.

Early the following morning, Heidi became suddenly alert but did not bark. We felt her body tense up and woke to find ourselves looking straight into the eyes of a huge buck with a giant head of antlers—one of the largest we had ever seen.

The buck stood at the foot of our sleeping bags, close to Heidi, checking us out. To Lenette and me, it felt like he was the spirit of the land. His land. Then, lifting his enormous head, he turned and disappeared into the forest. At that moment, we felt accepted and welcomed. During the entire encounter, Heidi remained silent. I'm sure she felt it, too.

That day we enjoyed wonderful hikes to every corner and felt welcomed. We knew we belonged, and that it was meant to be. All of it. We were home.

Lenette's Vision

03 August 2020

We went to Las Vegas to bring to life a dream Lenette had about a "Youth Hotel." Long story short, we made it happen, creating a company called Youth Systems Unlimited. Name the type of youth program, and we were committed to its creation, innovation, and excellence.

Soon we were doing government studies, designing, staffing, and operating children's programs for large apartment developments and national corporations. Various organizations contracted us to research children's programs and, where feasible, design and operate them. We studied and developed children's programs in Fiji and in many states across the U.S., including Hawaii.

A major hotel being constructed in Las Vegas invited us to present our ideas about a children's program. Two major universities were also competing for the contract. But, after listening to their goals, I submitted a three-page proposal titled "Instant Involvement." In essence, I stated that the children and their parents were accustomed to the best care and likely had their own swimming pools, tennis courts, and horses.

Entertaining them with games and stuff was wasted on them; they would tire quickly and soon return to their parents or caregivers for attention. We suggested that human connection was how to attract children and keep them interested and occupied. Staff who were trained to relate on a personal level was key. Activities would flow from establishing close relationships with each child. Naturally, we secured the contract.

Lenette designed the Youth Hotel, and we staffed it with fifty young college students and teachers who we trained and trained and trained! I write this with sincere pride: UNESCO recognized our program as the world's finest example of child care! Yet, it was what we always did.

Closing of Camp Letter
04 November 1970

1590 RAINDANCE
LAS VEGAS, NEVADA 89109

Dear Parents and Campers of our Many Wonderful Summers:

Camp Shasta is closing — well, not the site, that will continue in one form or another, but Camp Shasta, the idea, the method is dosed.

It is with mixed emotions that we do this since so much good has come to so many, and it is regrettable that we have no measuring device to accurately chart the values of our many Shasta Summers.

Has Camp changed anyone? Unlikely, and of course, this was never its intention. Has Camp contributed to one's growth? An unequivocal yes — physical — social — and emotional; Camp was more than anything else a catalyst to what we are all about.

Hiding behind anything proved impossible at Camp, so we all came to accept ourselves for what we are, not what we fantasized. Idolized images were shattered, and over the long run, we saw clay feet and wings too.

I guess that in many ways, Camp Shasta was way ahead of its contemporaries; not deliberately, but that is the way it happened. Today and more tomorrow, camps are becoming as Shasta, i.e., the individual in relation to a group; the group a cohesive family, and from this, viable unique individual growth and development.

When we at Camp said, "Do your own Thing," we finished by adding, "in relation to others." It is the relatedness we sought — and have for twenty years. Kids today say,

"Do your own thing," they don't mean it, and neither do they understand it. Rather than putting it all together, they confuse themselves; but by adding the cohesiveness of belonging, the "in

23

relation to others," it does come together because that is what it is all about and why Camp Shasta.

Regardless of who uses our site, they will do so calling their camp by any name they desire, but not "Camp Shasta." After all, what is in a name? Lots of memories.

We will keep all of you posted as to what the future holds for Camp Shasta, and in the meantime, if in your travels you visit Las Vegas, give us a call or drop us a line. Closing isn't all... Best of luck to everyone, camper, teenager, and parents, and a big warm Thank You.

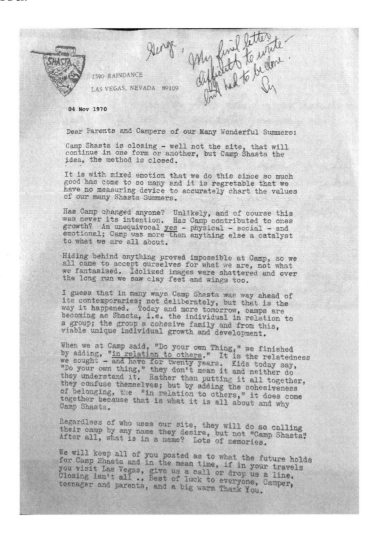

Las Vegas
07 August 2020

Our firm, Youth Systems Unlimited, continued to grow in line with the many responsibilities we had in the late 1960s and '70s. These included Camp Shasta, located in California, the Children's Campuses in Nevada and Denver, and the Youth Hotel in the Las Vegas International Hotel.

The Children's Campus was a free-standing community complex that met family needs for children from preschool through teens. Within large apartment developments in Las Vegas and Denver, they were designed by Lenette and under our management.

These preschools were an experiment the developers hoped would help promote apartment rentals to families. As it turned out, this was the primary reason families rented. The apartments filled more rapidly because of the excellence of the preschool, youth, and teen programs.

Our programs virtually eliminated crime and vandalism within the community. They proved so successful that they were deemed necessary for future developments at a national level. Yet, when U.S. interest rates climbed to almost 18%, all innovative programs and developments, particularly for families, came to a grinding halt.

Then, in the early '70s, Hilton Corporation purchased the International Hotel in Las Vegas. They replaced the knowledgeable leadership with their own Hilton-indoctrinated people. It did not take long before this proved to be a disaster, both for the Youth Hotel and ultimately for the Hilton Corporation's Las Vegas adventure.

When the new executive in charge informed me that anything I did would now require his approval. I quit, and the International Las Vegas Youth Hotel disappeared a year later. Ironically, they offered Lenette a designer position. Her reply: "Not a chance!"

The Olmec Heads
26 October 2022

In October 1974, we decided to go on an adventure to Mexico in our pop-top VW van. We even took some classes at Northridge College on the Pre-Columbian history of Mexico. Among graduate students, we both became the best students in the class. The professor knew we were planning an extensive trip to Mexico and intended to visit as many Pre-Columbian sites as we could. He warned us to be especially careful because we would be exploring areas not necessarily open to "gringos." It was typical of how we traveled, far from the beaten paths.

So, this is not a detail of our daily adventures, but of the strange events that began at dusk on a rainy night on the fringe of San Lorenzo south of Vera Cruz. We had begun looking for an off-road site to camp for the night when we saw several large Olmec Heads behind a wrought-iron fence. Because we had studied them as students, we immediately pulled over so we could walk the fence and see the Heads. The gate to the outdoor museum opened, and a tall man in a white shirt with rolled-up sleeves came out.

He said, "I was waiting for you. Come, and I will walk with you and tell the history of my heads." He was the museum's curator and, as we were to discover, so much more.

He took us on an amazing journey with a big flashlight. The Olmec Heads stood 6 feet high and were as wide as they were tall. During our "tour," Lenette and I watched in astonishment as the eyes of the heads appeared to follow us as we walked among them. The Olmec Heads seemed to come alive as he spoke; they were looking at us as we looked at them!

After the walk and talk, I invited him to join us for dinner in the village. Things became even stranger as we walked through the village. As it had stopped raining, people were coming out for the evening. As we passed by them, we saw the villagers offering our host the respect one might pay a king. They literally bowed as we walked by them.

We enjoyed a wonderful village dinner and a conversation about the history of the Mayans. I tried to pay, but no bill came, only smiles and outstanding service. Raul Mendez, spoke fluent English and probably ten other languages. Once dinner was over, we parted, but arranged to meet again in the morning for breakfast and more scintillating conversation. Wow, what an evening!

The following morning, we met at the café. We ate breakfast and again were not asked to pay. Raul invited us to his abode and told us he had some things to give us. He also asked to look at our map and where we planned to drive. His apartment was on the roof of the one small hotel in town. It was about twelve-foot square and contained a bed, washroom, small dresser, and a wire in the corner where two shirts and pairs of pants hung and nothing more. It was bare bones, but clean.

At that moment, we knew we had to send him some gifts like a radio, camera, books, and a shirt or two (and we did). Although a pauper by some standards, he was a king in the eyes of the villagers. We saw both in this one person. There was something truly remarkable about this man, and we felt it.

We returned to the café while he checked our map. He also gave Lenette a tiny piece of jade with a hole to string it. Raul said this was from Palenque and told us he was one of the archeological students on the dig with another student named Moises. He said Moises was a world-famous lecturer and teacher of Palenque history. He also said that they had not seen each other or talked in many years, but they were in touch. Before we asked how that could be, Raul said we were going to Palenque and showed us the only safe road to take, as other routes were not safe for us to travel. Also, he said we would arrive at night and meet Moises in the bar. We were locked in. People and events rule our lives.

When Raul gave the bit of jade to Lenette, he said, "This is from Palenque. It will watch over you." He then looked at me, put his finger to my heart, and said, "you have very important things to do, and Lenette must take care of you."

27

I didn't know then, but when we returned from Mexico, an entirely different life awaited us—a new chapter in my career working with professionals and entrepreneurs and a world of tremendous challenges.

Lenette wore the piece of jade around her neck, which had an extraordinary effect on those who saw it. Wherever we went, villagers, when they came close to her, all stepped back, not in fear but in awe. The tiny jade signified to the local Mayans that Lenette was an extremely important person. The jade was a message they all understood, but we did not, so Lenette decided to take off the necklace when we traveled among the locals.

A side story: When we tried to buy food from the food stands in the villages, we rarely paid for what we asked for. Whatever we chose was always met with smiles, a wave of the hands, and "No charge" in Spanish. We tried to pay but to no avail. We thoroughly enjoyed each moment of these experiences.

It was about 10:00 at night when we arrived in Palenque. The town was entirely dark except for a single light bulb shining in a store window, which turned out to be the bar in town. Having no other choice, we parked and went in.

It was empty, except for one man who invited us to sit. "Moises will be here shortly," he said in Spanish.

We waited about 10 minutes, and a little man walked in and came directly over to our table.

"Welcome to Palenque. My name is Moises, and I was expecting you," he announced in perfect English.

How did he know we were coming and would meet in this little bar? When we asked Moises if Raul had contacted him about us, he said they had not seen each other for many years and had not talked. So, if Raul did not call him, how did Moises know we were coming? Why did he come to the bar except to meet us? These were things we did not understand—and still don't.

Moises said that a French group hired him to guide them through Palenque and would be with them for the day. "Perhaps we can meet for dinner tomorrow evening?"

That or any other arrangement was fine with us, and we said so.

The next day we went to the site, ready for a full day of experiencing one of the great Mayan cities of its time. Who was waiting for us? With a big smile and welcome, it was Moises. He had asked another guide to take the French group so he could be with us for the day and evening.

Holy Mackerel, what more? Still, there was.

We cherished every moment of being expertly guided through the ruins by Moises. He spoke in great detail, sharing hundreds of wonderful stories about Palenque and its people. We were mesmerized by his every word as Moises continued into the evening.

Moises also mentioned that he was invited to lecture in many places. But, before he did, Moises would walk the streets in every new place he visited, and if the place did not feel good, he would fly home and not lecture.

"A place must welcome you," he said. "If not, leave it."

Moises told us we must go next to Casa Na Bolom, in San Crystaból, where archeologists Frans and Gertrude Duby Blom lived. Frans Blom was a famous archeologist studying the Mayans, and "Trudy" was a world-renowned photograpsher who came there to find him. She did, and they married. The two of them never stopped studying and caring for Mayans. At the Casa, rooms were always kept open and offered without cost to the Lacandon Maya who came to San Cristóbal for medical reasons.

Their hacienda was at the base of the stairway that led to a central plaza surrounded by totally white structures and a church. Below the small hill, the jungle overgrowth covered everything but the one road in and out.

We drove in, right up to their doorway, and when we knocked, someone came and said, "Welcome, we have been waiting for you. We have a room for you and dinner when you settle in."

Frans had passed away some years back, but spending time at the dinner table in Casa Na Bolom (*Na Bolom* means "Jaguar House" in the Tzotzil language) was nothing less than a miracle.

By now, we were used to going with the flow. It was all very surreal, but events dictated, and we were willing and excited to see where they took us. Why we've had these experiences and what meaning they have, if any, I do not ponder or worry about. Lenette and I can only be grateful for them all.

I walk on the ground
It is my reality
More above, below?

Living means using
No need to remind, I know
And do it fully.

On Our Way Home
11 November 2022

Before leaving San Crystaból, we were told that our journey home would take us through unsafe areas where bandits rule the roads. We heard that travelers in motor homes were killed, left hung on the highways, robbed, and molested. Still, we had no choice but to head north to the USA. Of course, much of our time was spent reliving our remarkably real, mind-bending experiences. No explanations, only a lot of thinking and talking.

Our drive north was uneventful until two fully armed bandits stepped out on a lonely road about a hundred miles from the border. They motioned with their sub-machine guns for me to pull over, and of course, I did. Lenette was still napping, so I slowly got out of the car. One man motioned me to the side of the road, and the other opened the door and put the gun to Lenette's head. She woke and became instantly aware of the situation. We both stayed remarkably calm, and since Lenette's Spanish was far better than mine, she asked what they wanted from us.

The one nearest Lenette replied, "Marijuana or pesos."

Ironically, we were leaving Mexico because we were running out of money. We had enough left for gas to return home. Lenette invited them to search the VW, explained that we had no marijuana, and showed them what little cash we had left. After one checked the VW, he found my Buck Knife, our only weapon. As the bandit examined it and fingered the blade, Lenette told him it was a gift from our son and important to me. He held it for a minute and looked us over. In those moments, I believe he considered killing us.

Smiling, he put the knife back where he found it and said, "Adios!"

Stunned but eager to leave, we quickly got back into our van and resumed our journey home, aware of how lucky we were. Serendipity? The word hardly does it justice! Or were we being watched over? In any event, it was a trip never to be forgotten.

Back To Big Changes
18 August 2020

We returned from Mexico mostly healed, having experienced wonderful people, culture, and country. What to do next became our immediate concern. We did not want to return to Las Vegas and quickly turned our existing programs over to those running them.

Clearly, we could not go backward, but only forward into the unknown. Historically, events ruled the direction we would take, so we waited for something to move us on. In the meantime, we needed to do something, so Lenette went to work in Incline Village, and I took a job at a casino resort in Reno.

It was not long after that I received a call asking if I could fill in for a speaker who fell ill. The subject was "Training Staff." The caller knew I had done this for twenty-seven-plus years. He felt I might have something to contribute to the professional group meeting at Lake Tahoe. This event turned into one that was life-changing.

They asked me to speak for an hour. When questions arose from the group of about fifty, we used up another two hours. It was challenging and exciting, and everyone felt the electricity in the room. When I left the podium, I was immediately surrounded by many participants asking if I'd visit and work with their staff. Holding staff training workshops was as natural to me as breathing. I felt I could do this in my sleep.

As a result, I flew to cities throughout the country and held all-day workshops for key people. During each workshop, something very significant became evident to me. The problems supposedly due to staff were rarely due to staff! It was the leader who was proving to be the problem. I was floored by this growing awareness.

This revelation motivated me to begin yet another journey. The research and study of leadership, power, and influence.

The 9th Symphony
08 June 2022

While at the computer, I decided for some reason to listen to Beethoven's 9th. I know this music from early childhood while sitting with my oldest brother, Peter, listening to the classical records he collected. I could have been five or less, but I clearly remember that he wanted me to listen with him whenever he bought a new record. I owe him much for that and more.

Beethoven and classical music, in general, have played a significant role in my life. It began with my brother Pete and continued well into my life. I recall the serendipitous moment on Okinawa when I cast a shadow on the tent of our company's captain. Beethoven's music drew me from my guard station to listen to a quartet he was playing on a wind-up record player. He, and the music playing at that moment, contributed to changing the path I was walking—and it was extraordinary.

Listening today brought tears to our eyes. I write "our" because Lenette heard the music, came into the office, and saw me sitting back and conducting with a pencil. She cried, and I teared up too, because this is what I used to do all the time. Another reminder that life goes on.

In my opinion, Beethoven wrote the monumental 9th Symphony for the world, not only for the Germanic people. It is literally an "Ode to Man" everywhere. It goes beyond genius in both the music and words. Besides moving me to tears, the 9th brings to mind the condition of our world today.

I grieve for the young of our world. I feel that technology alone does not hold the answer to the problems they will face in the days ahead. The importance of genuine communication cannot be overstated. Without it, meaningful solutions and relationships are impossible. The device in their hand won't hold any of the answers. Those will only be found in their heads and hearts.

My Memory Bank
21 June 2022

My memory bank is still operational and clear, and I continue to make withdrawals. Most of these memories are positive, and I view some of them as crossroads where choices were made. Some of these choices were mine, and some were not. Along the way, many events and people played essential roles in the directions my life took.

A brief example: I took and passed a test in high school to be placed in the Navy V5 program, which meant the possibility of being a fighter pilot and four years of college. It turned out that I am red and green colorblind, which kept me out of the program, so I joined the army. My desire to enter the war dictated my actions, so I quit high school and left for basic training. The rest of the story I've told.

All humans are subject to the pull and push of life. Some of us are lucky enough to be born and raised where the environment and our parents allow us opportunities galore to be what we choose. I grew up during a full-blown depression, living with my family in tight quarters. My siblings and I all looked forward to getting out of school, finding a job, and earning enough money to bring home with some left over to spend on small pleasures. The Second World War brought an abrupt end to the depression, and for those of us born in the U.S., opportunities exploded. If fate had decreed otherwise, I might have been born in a little Ukrainian village. But that's life and the luck of the draw.

Now, as I age well into the nineties, I conclude I am and have been a very lucky pup. I hope you feel this way about yourself.

Memories of past
Some good and some not so good
So life is lived

Haiku Thoughts

September 2021

Haiku is simple. The form is five syllables followed by seven syllables then five more. It attempts to paint a picture of the natural world using few words. I enjoy the 5-7-5 syllables form and use it to express anything and everything. I hope you will enjoy one or two.

Time has its own time
It unfolds at its own pace
Fast or slow, it goes

I read and I write
Work to fill a time with thought
It works then does not

This day is just fine
Sun, blue skies, mountains so clear
One of those sweet days

Often our state of world
Troubles me and I know zero
Or can do nothing

Nice to be in touch
Hearing from you is so good
Thank you for doing

This day is vital
How many more are left us?
Enjoy the moment

How lucky to be
I see, I hear, I feel now
What else do we need?

Time cannot be held
It is not a thing or place
Or river that flows

Enjoy each moment
It leaves too soon and now what?
Waiting is foolish

We are so unique
None the same and yet we try
Be yourself and glad

Words are a challenge
Be sure of how you use them
Oft misunderstood

Nature offers so much
Try saying this as Haiku
be original

Aging is a fact
Do not run away from it
Helpless, in any case

What gifts they arranged
Virginia City
Lake Tahoe, blue sky, and rain

Other time other guests
Family they are to us
How blessed to share time

Family, not blood
We have this with each other
And stories galore

Our history full
Plus memories of people
Rich experience

Grateful is easy
We see the bright side of things
A choice that we make

Time is limited
We must make the most of it
Be kind, be caring

Share you with others
Anticipate needs, fill them
Be a gift to them

Discrimination
Why this and hatred one has
What is taught, how else?

Getting old happens
No avoiding taking place
What do you do then?

This day is yours now
It will be gone in a flash
Enjoy each moment

"Pandemic" the name
How do we care for our self?
Being there for each

ON RELATIONSHIPS

The Challenges Facing Human Relationships

31 May 2021

Every human relationship faces challenges. We are each unique, and so how we communicate tests our differences. Are we willing and able to have genuine dialogue that accepts our differences, or will we insist on agreement with our singular position? Consider the differences between people with different political and religious beliefs. Because of these differences, is communication or dialogue possible, or if not, is this problem one that could eventually destroy our relationships?

Our differences may not be imposing stone walls, but we must acknowledge that they exist. And if we accept this, can we recognize that we can disagree with each other and still feel heard and understood? If so, how likely are we to learn something from each other?

Our life experiences create our perspectives on how we see, hear, feel, and think. Often we are generations apart. Do we expect grandparents and grandchildren to understand each other's views only because they have blood in common? Those who grow and live in one generation cannot know what the other has experienced except through what they are told and have read.

Love and acceptance are essential first steps to understanding each other. Only then can we know about the unique experiences that have shaped our lives and our viewpoints. We must all take the opportunity to learn more about how we've arrived at where we are and what we believe, even if agreement isn't possible.

Belief vs. Fact

24 May 2021

It takes two at a minimum to dialogue, but what if only one is open to experiencing it? When it comes to dialogue, all involved in that moment of conversation must adhere to the fundamental rules which make dialogue possible. Parties are mentally present, receptive, and respectful. The listener strives to understand what is being said and asks questions if they do not.

Entirely absent from these few hard and fast rules is any agreement to agree—unless the parties accede to that before the dialogue begins. In practice, this is a rare occurrence. In some circumstances, people are unwilling to concede that their positions are open to challenge or dispute. They may not see their thoughts and words as beliefs, but as facts. If this is the case, any attempt to argue is futile.

In those extreme situations, the parties are now faced with a decision about how to proceed: agree to disagree and maintain the relationship or break it apart. I suggest the choice must be based on the historical relationships between those involved. Emotion aside, being able to step away from conflict and agreeing to disagree is a deeply personal issue. And for some, extremely complicated, harking back to family and the "kitchen table."

It is easy to picture a young family in a discussion around the dining table or in the living room. Yet, in many cases, the conversation was a monologue. Often the father's or mother's words were heard and no one else's. Argument or disagreement was never an option for those who weren't invited to participate or voice their opinions; unquestioning acceptance was expected.

When people communicate as equals, acceptance can never be guaranteed. Although we all have beliefs, we do not have all the hard facts. It's important not to confuse the two.

"For those who believe, no proof is necessary. For those who don't believe, no proof is possible." Stuart Chase.

Too Many Questions, Too Few Answers

14 December 2012

The world is in a precarious place. Many families and individuals are facing their own challenges here in our own country. Politically, our country has split over issues that appear to be intransigent. Is there a possible solution that might address all of this? In my own very insignificant opinion, I believe the problem at the heart of these issues is one of communication. I'm not referring to news media, cell phones, or the thousands of social apps, but old-fashioned face-to-face dialogue.

We can improve how we interact by listening, understanding what the other is saying, and confirming what we've heard. While we don't need to agree, we do need to convey our genuine understanding with a modicum of empathy.

The amount of information delivered to our devices is massive. While it has value in being available to everyone, it is wrong to mistake data for truths. And it can't be compared with one's "hands-on experiences."

Hearsay, including the avowed testimony of others, is not part of our own experience. Those who relate the words and supposed experiences of others as their own truths are, in fact, mere gossip mongers. They don't say, "I was told" or "I read." Instead, they say, "I know." This although no one can know what they have not personally experienced.

We as a culture and society are in deep trouble, and I strongly believe this has much to do with the limited amount of time we spend face to face. We need to touch, see, hear, and understand each other. Many do not gather to eat together or meet to share the day and their thoughts and feelings.

How and in what way do we "communicate?" Is e-mailing, texting, or talking on our cell phones good enough? And do we dare miss escaping into our favorite television or streaming programs depicting life as we are not living it?

We have always held up the family unit as the strength and heart of our country. Yet, who can seriously believe this today? How many families sit at the kitchen table together for dinner, intent on hearing and understanding the words and stories each has and wants to tell without media and cell phone interference? Do we define work by meetings that do not occur in the same room? And if they do, are people engaged in dialogue or being lectured to on firm agendas? We as a society have to ask ourselves where and when do spontaneous and creative interactions between people occur?

Plainly, there are more questions than answers. Still, those of us who take the time to enjoy genuine dialogue with our families, associates, and significant others are truly blessed.

Times Like Today
28 Apr 2020

Challenging times bring with them events that, whether we like it or not, exert a tremendous influence on our lives. This is what most face today, yet these and the experiences they bring with them hold important lessons. In difficult times, the need to learn from confronting our emotional, physical, and material challenges is more critical than ever.

If we are present enough to recognize negative and positive events as an opportunity to grow, they have much to offer. Especially if we wish to be better prepared for what may come.

When one refuses to learn, it becomes a loss for them and, ultimately, for those they interact with. Even in the usual day-to-day events, it is vital to recognize their potential value. If one doesn't, can't, or won't, they stand to gain nothing and lose much.

Events, including the ones we are likely to ignore, are what drive us to make the choices we do, even those concerning our relationships with others. While we can nurture relationships we feel good about and cut off those we don't, there are exceptions. Working with a controlling boss is a good example. If it's how we make a living, we do what we have to protect ourselves and our income source. Financial necessity is the event that dictates the importance of the relationship, so we do what's necessary to maintain it. Even so, most marriages of convenience are doomed to fail once events dictate otherwise.

Being Open
28 October 2014

Our growth takes root when we are honest, respectful, nurturing, and accepting of ourselves and the people closest to us. At birth, all humans are open and vulnerable but soon begin to abandon the process of being themselves. Instead, they become what others in power influence them to be. Therefore, to a considerable degree, we learn to be what others choose for us.

If loving, nurturing, and accepting, we will remain ourselves. Still growing, being, and becoming—but always our unique selves and not what others would have us be. On the other hand, if the influence of those who hold power over us is harmful, whether unconscious or intentional, we will become what we must in order to survive. Yet, this is learned behavior, which can be unlearned, regardless of how deep it goes. We can't change what we inherit, but we can overcome what we've been wrongly taught.

Still, it takes courage to be open and vulnerable. All of us can appear open, but appearance is an act that we believe hides us and therefore fools others. Yet, those closest to us are never fooled. They know the truth of who and what we really are. We rarely look inward, spending most of our time looking outward and believing what we "see" in the mirror.

Being open to the objectivity of others close to us is never easy to experience. One must deal with the fear that their weaknesses will be exposed. And it also means surrendering power to those speaking their truth, even if only temporarily.

Not surprisingly, it is the most powerful among us who need to embrace their vulnerability and invite those important to them to communicate how they are perceived and "known." These can be dangerous grounds to stand on without a knowledgeable mentor to facilitate and foster honest mutuality, authentic interaction, and dialogue. Real growth and change begin deep within. It can only happen when what is outside is allowed in.

Two To Tango
28 April 2019

Each of us is different in small but significant ways. Even identical twins witness the world from a unique place within themselves. The mixing of what is inherited and experienced with people and events makes us different. This reality contributes to our individuality; what we are now, and what we are to become. Nothing is exactly what it was a moment ago. Life challenges us with a barrage of people and events pushing and pulling us toward unknowns we cannot know until we get there. Like a lump of clay, we are constantly molded by forces beyond our ability to control, such as aging. These changes are actual, not potential. Still, the degree of change depends on our experiences and how we incorporate them. Here, so much relies on our courage and vulnerability to others and events. How else do we learn?

If we take the time to know ourselves as we are on this day, we can only discover this from and through our meaningful relationships. It is the other that knows us as objectively as we do them. It's the only way we'll know if we are good partners, parents, teachers, students, leaders, employees, and friends. Still, we'll never find out without genuine dialogue, authentic respect, and trust.

It takes "Two to Tango," a dance that demands some intricate and exotic moves from both parties involved. And so it is with relationships. We are either in step or out of step with others. Doing the dance as it needs to be danced with significant others is essential. Either a coordinated dance blends two or more into creative and productive relationships, or there is confusion, stumbling, and conflict. In important relationships, it takes little to see, feel, and know the difference between the harmonious and the dysfunctional. No one in the dance is fooled.

Everyone's journey has to do with actualizing one's self. That is, being as fully one's self as possible. This journey is rarely easy and certainly not a solo endeavor. It requires others, starting at conception and taking us into whatever life has in store for us. Our first lesson starts with our parents; then, formally or otherwise, continues with the others we interact with as we mature. The wiser among us seek to learn and allow experiences and others to enter our very being. Only then are we able to "Tango."

Differences vital
Experience and others
Essential to us

Am I successful?
A question I must answer
Since truth is within

Do I dance alone?
It does take Two to Tango
Completes the picture

Consequences

21 January 2021

Every act we perform has consequences. Some are meaningless and pass us by. At other times, consequences are so significant that they bring about life-changing events. If fully present, we are aware of what is taking place. We see, hear, and possibly understand its implications. If this is the case, we may actually alter the outcome of what is taking or is about to take place.

In an ancient story, God declares loudly and clearly that a tsunami is coming and for all to seek higher ground. One person, not mentally present, misses the message, but another who is present hears and understands and flees to safety. These two experience the same event but with different consequences for each.

How many thousands of years have humans possessed the ability to be fully in the moment? How else can we hear the message, understand its implications, and potentially alter the consequences? Consider (once again) the importance of talk at the kitchen table. Children witness and learn from their parents—but do they understand? If not, repercussions occur based on ignorance and misunderstanding. Do those events repeat throughout our lives? I believe they do.

Over the years of teaching leaders, I've seen the consequence of poor leadership. When leaders treat their followers as things, they respond in kind, with negative results. Anyone related to in this manner knows what they experience. How does a lousy leader realize they are the root cause of sickness in their relationships? They do not. Instead, they fault others.

Do you want the best possible interactions with those you live and work with? Be authentic, treat people with respect as equals and empower and nurture at every opportunity. When problems arise—and they will—view them as the learning experiences they are and use them to stimulate dialogue and creativity and increase the likelihood of rewarding outcomes.

The Challenges Of Communication
27 March 2021

Relationships are essential to life. They bring us together, forming families and friendships and creating organizations, cities, states, and countries. In the process of establishing relationships, we communicate—and our communication brings us together. Without communication, how else could this occur? And yet, historically, there has always been agreement and disagreement between individuals and countries.

The highest level of communication between two or many is genuine dialogue. This calls for respecting the other, being present, listening and understanding what is being said, and asking questions for clarification.

When this is achieved, the conditions described switch to the listener, who now becomes the speaker. During this exchange, there is no leader or follower for those moments. Clearly, that condition alone challenges leaders accustomed to being in charge and followers accustomed to acceding to the leader's demands.

Note that this process has nothing to do with agreement. Expecting agreement without asking for it upfront creates a dilemma. Stating the need for agreement at the beginning of dialogue is the better choice, but that's still problematic—as it may be an impossible request.

In today's world, we see communication breakdowns in families and between dear friends, co-workers, associates, and within organizations and nations. This challenges the best of relationships, and I offer no simple answer. The problem usually manifests when opinions are expressed as facts. Religion, politics, child-rearing, and education are examples of issues that often bring conflict and even pain when and where people talk.

Again, I mention the kitchen table as the likely source of many implanted beliefs and prejudices. When genuine dialogue fails and monologue takes the stage, it is a loss to all parties. Yet, that happens all too often.

Speaking The Truth
19 April 2021

So, where is the truth? In these times, the amount of information is mind-boggling. Click or swipe your cell phone, and the information you seek appears instantly at your fingertips. Is that information guaranteed to be truth or merely digital hearsay? How can we tell one from another? While there is no simple answer to that question, I can tell you that "alternative facts" do not exist.

Then, how do we know truth? We know it through experience. We know it by being there, seeing it, and swimming in it. It's not in our imagination or what we read or heard from someone telling us what they believe to be true. Truth is truth—not what we want or wish. Truth demands courage and must be expressed in its naked form and never sugarcoated or dumbed down.

Still, there are many problems associated with speaking truth, which is why it's challenging to be truthful. Often, truth may not be what others want to hear or accept. The person speaking may believe what they say is true, regardless of whether it is speculation or hearsay. If the speaker expects the listener to agree with or accept what was said, they will usually be disappointed. In any genuine dialogue, all must accept that non-agreement is part of being open and honest.

But then again, if we aren't listening to each other, how important is the truth anyway?

I see you, but hear?
Maybe yes and maybe no
Do we care which one?

Why do we argue?
We may disagree, why not?
At least we listen

Being Creative With Relationships

18 October 2021

Creativity, even attempting to be creative, means going where you haven't been before. After all, the beauty of creativity is discovery. In the context of relationships, it might mean doing and saying something you haven't done or said before. Ralph Waldo Emerson said, "All life is an experiment. The more experiments you make, the better."

That resonates with me because of my history with ideas and people. Years back, I experimented with children's behavior, creating a positive environment that enabled them to grow and achieve their potential. They could move on from being what they thought others wanted them to be and instead be more themselves. I discovered that if children felt safe being themselves, they were also more willing to be open and receptive in their relationships with others. The ability to be authentic directly affects whether an individual will become more trusting and open, or more closed and restrictive.

While certain experiences bring us together, we still need to discover and experiment with what brings us greater awareness and appreciation of the people we interact with. I have always believed we are here for each other and for ourselves at the same time.

We all benefit when we create opportunities and experiences within our relationships to better understand each other. In striving to keep our experiences positive, we grow from those authentic interactions. Otherwise, we miss that opportunity.

Simply knowing that we are different and similar at the same time isn't enough. Being able to experience and value that is what's important. Indeed, the creative application of authentic dialogue plays an essential part in this. Each of us has the potential to be more open and truer to ourselves. To be what others want us to be is a loss to all.

I am me to be
So I choose being myself
We both benefit

Let me be myself
Better for both, this is best
Being you and me

Power In Relationships

30 March 2022

Power is not thought of as an aphrodisiac by accident. Like sex, it rewards the power holder's brain with dopamine and other chemical jolts. The way abusive power achieves its goals is by exploiting one's fear of consequences. Our life experiences, whether real or perceived, significantly contribute to the fear of power.

Ultimately, power needs to be exercised responsibly, especially in relationships. I believe that only one person initiates how a relationship and the associated environment develop. That in itself constitutes leadership, even if one does not see or accept themselves as a leader. When the power to control exists in a relationship, it must be used in ways that those without this power will feel safe. Building a mutually rewarding relationship will be impossible if the power holder abuses it to diminish others.

The positive uses of power cannot be overstated. The concepts of positive leadership, personal empowerment, and responsibility were central to Camp Shasta's philosophy. And it was successful in every aspect. Yet not all saw it that way. In the sixties, a parent, a professor of psychology, spent a week at camp studying our philosophy and application. She saw how the camp experience deliberately built responsibility into each child. Still, she questioned this because, in her view, once the campers returned home, they would be seen and treated in their previous roles: Children needing care from their parents and teachers.

Of course, our view was quite different. We never treated children as needing care at camp. Instead, we empowered them to care for themselves and gave them the tools to realize their potential. Year after year, we learned that their growth did not go unnoticed. And, as those children became young adults, most became what camp fed them. As aging witnesses to this, we're thrilled.

Is Being Yourself Ever Really Being Just You?

09 April 2022

The more I write about self and relationships, the more I sense we are never just ourselves. My history clearly shows my brothers, sister, and parents' influences on me. I am not them, to be sure, but I am not without them in one way or another.

We are multiple beings who meet life each day. We are not unlike an orchestra with various instruments meant to be in harmony with each other while connected to its conductor. This arrangement may also bring conflict, whether or not conscious, between those who want to be dominant and others who also wish to play this role.

For years, I taught people to be themselves. The idea that multiple selves exist within us was one that never entered my mind. Now, for the first time, it does because I am an old man searching my past. As I do so, I've become more aware than ever before that I am a product of my history. Mostly, this is not my doing, but as a result of my family and the environment in which we co-existed.

Creating a constructive environment is one of the ways a leader can help and nurture others. I ensured that people under my power and influence had the time and space to be the same person as often as possible. I was always aware that while with others, they may have struggled to be their best selves or resumed previous roles related to their past environments.

Many of the most painful experiences are continuous, and navigating beyond the emotional muck and mire is extremely difficult, even with the best help. Still, only after we free ourselves from those painful environments and influences can we be our best selves.

I am me, or who?
I will not be my brothers
And not my parents

Power And Influence
07 June 2021

Power and influence are potentially strong emotional issues. Depending on how used and interpreted, they can grow or diminish a person. I've trained those in positions of power to empower those they lead so that growth is the chosen path, creating a sense of ownership and improved participation.

On the other hand, where is the benefit of treating people like things and making them feel insignificant? How one feels profoundly influences their behavior. To believe feelings have nothing or little to do with relationships is to miss much of what brings and holds people together.

My research and hands-on work have shown that communication is clearly the problem confronting all the answers we seek between us. Those who use their power wisely know that feelings have much to do with people's behavior. When we respect and take the time to understand each other's thoughts and feelings, the likelihood of a positive and productive relationship increases.

When those in power use power and influence to satisfy their own needs, they assume agreement or consensus is unnecessary. This negative attitude harms the relationship and the job to be done.

The leader who listens, understands, confirms their followers, and earnestly seeks consensus throughout their relationships and discussions wins—as do their followers. Powerful people that nurture good feelings in those they lead will share the benefits.

Why Dialogue Is Important To Me

25 June 2022

When I write, I write what I feel and think at the moment. Still, it is nothing more than my opinion. My history, in large part, is why I continue to write on the subject of dialogue. I think its lack is at the root of many relationship problems. For some leaders, communication is often a mere monologue. Conversely, for some followers, not being mentally present when others attempt to communicate is just as problematic. Under these circumstances, little or nothing of value can occur between them.

My engagement with dialogue began at an early age. At home, and being the fifth in line, I could only observe as my siblings and parents talked or yelled at or over each other. I hated the arguments that inevitably ensued. When that happened, I ran to be with my friends, where plain talk was valued. Not surprisingly, I preferred the conversational exchanges I had with my peers. As far as I was concerned, that was a far better form of communication. And in my opinion, genuine dialogue takes a conversation to the next level.

I speak and you hear
You speak and I understand
We get along fine

Genuine Communication Is Never Easy

12 August 2022

When speaking to those close to you as a parent, leader, teacher, friend, or acquaintance, does your voice and behavior show less than respect and regard for them? This is an important question to ask yourself because how you communicate and with what intent is heard and understood loudly and clearly. People will respond accordingly. Is this what any reasonably good leader wants? I think not. Yet, this is a common occurrence in hierarchical relationships. The one in power is responsible for the relationships under their influence. It is the way it is.

Whoever is at the top of the pyramid is responsible for making every relationship they have with those below them work for all. When those in power communicate clearly and authentically, everyone benefits. If not, or perceived as not, then seeds of discontent manifested through behavior are assured.

Forms of hierarchy are ubiquitous and exist in almost every relationship. It could be due to intelligence, strength, abilities, age, or any combination of these factors. It's everywhere—in homes, schools, and most certainly at work; in fact, where does it not exist? The art of outstanding leadership is making it seem to disappear.

ON SELF

Our Journey To Self-Actualization
15 May 2019

From birth, being one's self is not easy. The road we each travel to attain degrees of self is challenging and often dangerous. And what road exists may disappear along the way. What then, when there is no path to follow?

So much depends on those who gave us life and the environment we were born into. The cards we are dealt are full of unknowns until we make a few of our own choices. In the process, how often do we dare to challenge the unknown? Regrettably, too many people remain fixed in places where they age and eventually die.

Those fortunate enough to have parents who can afford to provide them with mentors, an excellent education, and a variety of experiences have the advantage of those resources. They are much more likely to grow beyond who they were and potentially give to others.

Compare this to many others with limited means. Growing up with few resources and experiences deprives people of the tools needed for growth and diminishes their desire to do for others. Caring for one's own basic needs is usually all those with limited resources can do. Here, one's potential "to be" is restricted. Not only are they likely destined to do poorly, but this is also society's loss.

If not from experience, where does growth come from? Aging is unavoidable, but one can age without growth. Growth demands our willing participation. Do books and teachers have the same power to influence us compared to personal experiences? Without question, experience has the greater power. Experience not only induces growth, but it also demands that we "pay our dues." These dues are directly related to the degree of awareness and openness to what we are experiencing.

Learning is not automatic. Only the courageous among us draw lessons from experiences. This is why many of our experiences (wars, deteriorating environment, disease, etc.) are repeated endlessly. Humans either learn and grow from experience or remain stuck, and the journey to actualize is denied. The loss of anyone's potential must be considered a loss to everyone.

Unless held hostages by certain illnesses, people know where they have been; know where they are, and where they are going. Life is generally composed of expected events, but the unexpected happens frequently. And those with limited experience can rarely deal well with the unexpected. Worse, nothing is learned.

Those blessed with self-actualizing opportunities are far better prepared. When adversity strikes, they are equipped to deal with it. They know to be immediately present and open to the unexpected and learn from the lessons which occur. If societies could facilitate self-actualization for one and all, the potential benefits would be enormous.

Self is that unique
Nothing is duplicated
Each of us special

I continue growth
What stops me is you or me
But I choose which one

Events do happen
Is value found within them?
Lessons are in most things

Society vs. The Individual

22 April 2020

We are each unique and must do all we can to maintain and enrich our specialness. At the same time, we must also be part of what we call "society." Both are demanding challenges that begin early in our lives, and rarely are these two opposing forces receptive to cooperation.

Uniqueness comes first to us, and at its roots, it is never diminished. Yet, society is so powerful that its influence begins its task of shaping each of us very early in our life. It's almost a hopeless battle as society, led by our parents, family, teachers, friends, and leaders, pressures us to become what they have in mind for us to be.

If our immediate teachers honor their own uniqueness, they will nurture this in their children. In this event, what comes naturally is strengthened, and the child becomes more themselves than what society expects of them. If, on the other hand, our initial teachers are themselves attached to society to the point where their uniqueness is mostly non-existent, they will force this upon their children. Not surprisingly, the children will become their parents.

Being unique as an individual is not a serious societal problem unless they live so far outside of society's boundaries that what they do and how they live endangers those around them. Today, the considerable danger of the covid virus is encircling the world. All countries are taking precautions that severely restrict their populations. Among these are mask mandates, social distancing, and many others. Schools, businesses, restaurants, etc., are closed.

The entire world is at risk, so its societies are reacting. Individuals are being told what to do and how to live. Society at large has imposed restrictions on those who would fight for their independence and uniqueness, but instead must adhere to what society demands.

It is more likely that those who have given in to not being themselves as children will adapt quickly. Compliance will be more difficult for those who have fought dearly for their individual rights. Still, despite their reluctance to comply, they should be present enough to recognize the reasoning behind what society is asking of them. Those who will not suffer the consequences.

There is a time for individual rights to be fought for. And there is a time when adhering to practices to promote the common good is also required. Living in a world with others makes it necessary for all people to care for each other.

Why do we not learn?
Experience is our gift
If we learn from it

I need to be me
You need to be you, also
Why not help others

Unique is a gift
So give it to one and all
More where that comes from

Changing Times
07 May 2020

Most people probably realize that our world is changing, but into what we can only guess.

For me, it is only a watching game. If this pandemic had happened during my working and creative times, I would have been without work and the wonderful people I worked with. I also wonder if I would have been the student I was—researching, studying, and applying what I knew and learned about leadership, power, and dialogue? Most likely the answer is, yes.

I always placed demands on myself. Even as a kid, working to earn a penny was essential, and as my entrepreneurial spirit grew, so did my need to have others join me. As luck would have it, my endeavors prospered and grew in many ways. How blessed we were to have lived in times where zero could be turned into something substantial.

As of this writing, the entire world is experiencing difficult and demanding events. There are no straightforward answers. In fact, no answers at all as of yet. As I've always thought and said, events rule. Good leaders pay attention to this and learn and act accordingly. Bad and ineffective leaders allow their egos to rule their behavior, and any significant lessons are ignored. Now, more than ever, the world needs good leaders.

We Each Are Who We Are
08 June 2020

We each are who and what we are. You and I are not the same. None of us are the same, and I believe that's a good thing. We benefit from our differences the same way spices enrich and enhance what they are mixed with. I do not ask that you respect me first, but know that I respect you and your uniqueness. In the process, I certainly hope you respect me, too. We both benefit when we share our ideas and beliefs—even if we disagree. I have no problem with you whether we agree or not.

I need to thank you for what you have given me. You do so just by being. I hope you benefit from my uniqueness as I do from yours. Differences are the gifts we bring to each other. Be a giver of you and a receiver of the other. I am so much more than I would be because of you.

Events Are Experiences

27 March 2020

I stumbled on this piece of insight many years ago while leading a workshop and instantly realized its value. The realization that if not present—a common state of most people—what is missed is the call, the knock at the door, the event that brings us the potential for learning something new. It might even be the answer we have been seeking. Never to be taken for granted, events are experiences that may or may not have important messages that teach. So how do we benefit if we are not entirely present and open to the message?

The demand that we be present in the "here and now" has been around for as long as humanity has. Prehistoric man had to learn and apply or die. Learning the skills to survive had to be paramount, which was why almost any event had to be viewed as a "learning experience." I suppose that if the majority of prehistoric people were like most of us today, many were caught and eaten. The rare ones learned to survive and became mentors, sharing their survival insights with others. Is this how leadership initially evolved?

I call experience an event and emphasize it as an opportunity to learn and apply valuable lessons. Some events might offer little, but others can be life-changing, such as the current pandemic.

Today, our world is caught in a major event. Are we learning the lessons it offers, or are we lost in worrying about our tomorrows? My plea is to do everything possible to stay present and squeeze every lesson we can from it. This is a time to learn and apply, not to run into the morass of "what will be?"

We need to survive this day so we can better meet the future and what it may bring. We can't spend our time worrying and planning. It is this day we must survive and, in the process, take all we can from it so that we can make our world better and safer.

Candid: Is There A Better Way To Be?

27 November 2020

How important is your truth? What is your truth? Why is being yourself so important? If you are not yourself, who are you? What do you say if you do not say what you want to say? These questions, and many more like them, should not be taken lightly. They directly point to whether we are ourselves at this moment or are being what others want us to be.

If we are ourselves, we speak candidly, not to harm or to disagree. This is always possible with those we communicate with when we express ourselves openly and honestly. We also invite and actually insist that others speak their own voice. This is what makes for our best leaders and role models. They speak authentically and do their best to empower the same in those they relate to.

All of our own truths are too important to hide. Yet, if we expose our truth, do we jeopardize our place at the "kitchen table" at school or at work? This is a serious problem to overcome, which is why good leadership is essential to our being open in conversations. Quality leadership provides a role model inviting and seeking genuine dialogue, making us feel safe and secure.

A brief story: The relationship I had with the president of the International Hotel was an honest and open one, and our program for children prospered. We listened to and understood each other. When the property was sold to the Hilton Corporation, they replaced the original leader with their own corporate man. In little time, he clarified he did not want dialogue with his subordinates, only adherence to his policies. "I raised three boys, and I know all about children. I will instruct you."

The choice between being a pawn and self was easy. I quit, and a year later, the children's program closed. This was a loss never to be recovered.

A Desire To Grow

10 December 2020

A desire to grow and to go beyond oneself needs to come from inside us. We decide whether to be open and vulnerable to the experiences life throws at us. We choose to either be a willing participant or closed off from what we hear and experience. Having arms twisted and minds forced open does not make for receptivity. Others close to us may sincerely want this of us, believing it is for our own good. Yet, unless this comes from within us, efforts by others are wasted. It is not what others want of us, but what we want of ourselves.

My workshops are classic examples. I know I prepared what I believed was valuable material. To prepare for the workshop, I gathered relevant history, philosophy, and psychology. I also knew that creating the safest possible environment was my responsibility, and I needed to do everything I could to make this a reality. One way was to not push people to share their thoughts and feelings. If one chose to remain silent, they were respected for this. They would pick their own time to share or not share their thoughts.

It was not what I said and did that made any difference. It was the receptivity that each individual brought to those moments. I could only know if they were closed or resistant to what I shared by engaging them in dialogue. Acceptance of where each participant was at became my most successful approach. When people were ready to speak their minds, they did, and I confirmed them without judging them.

My goal was to create an environment of trust, respect, and understanding. When feelings that are always so personal and unique began to be shared and listened to without judgment, individuals spoke what they felt and thought. This opened up even the most reluctant. Only after they felt safe could they find the courage to express themselves.

As a result, people opened up to each other. In fact, I often received letters and calls before a workshop asking that certain subjects be discussed before I presented what I had prepared. I never stood in the way of this; after all, that was the entire point.

I speak my own mind
And want to hear this from you
We say what we say

I am truth each day
I seek truth in every way
Please be only you

Are You A Leader?
30 January 2021

So, are you a leader? Do you want to be one? If you are a leader or aspire to be, I suggest you look at yourself in the mirror and ask, "Am I myself, or am I an act?"

The best leaders excel at being themselves. To be an outstanding leader, you must set exceptional examples for those you lead in as many ways as possible. Your behavior and words must be authentic when interacting with those around you. Always be aware you are a role model to those closest to you. Just as importantly, you must serve your followers if they are to serve you.

Also, understand the followers who serve you do so for a variety of reasons. Therefore, being authentic, caring, and respectful in your actions and interactions will increase the likelihood that they will serve you as well as you serve them. Good leaders nurture their followers to grow and ultimately meet or exceed their potential.

Of course, we have all experienced leaders with no sense or desire to serve anyone other than themselves. These are those who love the power and influence they can exert over others. Those who follow this leader do so for many reasons; some are attracted by their own love of power, whether directly or by association. Rarely can they accomplish what they are truly capable of since they remain solely for their own benefit.

So, for good or bad, it does not matter whether one seeks, takes, makes, or is given the role to lead. The demands on all leaders are identical when it comes to influencing the behavior of their followers. The raw necessities the good leader must possess are attitude, behavior, and the ability to communicate with those they lead. Conversely, the poor leader who lacks these qualities and who either underestimates or does not understand their importance is left to ponder why problems and difficulties with their followers persist.

An exemplary leader also recognizes that leadership exists within any group with a common goal or undertaking. Among these are those who lead or seek to lead, but there are also others who are reluctant to step into a leadership role for reasons of their own. They are potentially capable of leadership, but prefer to only do their job and fulfill their responsibility as good team players. Usually, these people are outstanding at what they do, including having excellent relationships with those they work and live with. Although they might not accept taking on any leadership roles, they serve and support those close to them. By their actions and words, they already possess the authentic attributes of leadership. A good leader would do well to recognize and reward that individual, as it benefits the organization by fostering initiative and inspiring like behavior in others.

Leaders are defined by their actions and words, both good and bad. Those close to them can clearly see and know them for who they really are — regardless of what the leader believes themself to be. Interacting daily with powerful individuals makes it impossible not to know them, often better than they know themselves. They are not kings who can hide behind their elegant clothes. Instead, whether or not they choose to be transparent, they will reveal their true selves and, in the end, reap what they sow.

I believe leaders emerge in every group endeavor and that leadership is a natural phenomenon. Without talented leaders, humanity might not have been able to survive. Leadership is what made it possible for people to live in groups.

Good leaders, bad leaders, and those who follow are dynamic roles that constantly change as people emerge from among us to fill them. Each of us possesses these qualities, whether from natural propensity or learned behavior, as they are a foundational part of the human experience.

Lead me to be me
And I lead others to be
How important is self?

Bureaucracy And System
13 March 2021

I watched the interview with Prince Harry and Meghan, and it stirred up some concerns I have had for many years. Those are the issues of bureaucracy and the visible and invisible barriers created by them.

When I personally or my organizations bumped into bureaucracy, I backed off. I will freely share that my being ruled and restricted by administrators or systems never sat well with me. When it happened—and I am sure it did, I walked away if I could. If not, such as in school, military service, etc., I did what had to be done to the best of my abilities, but made little noise and stayed in the shadows. Clearly, being myself and following my own tune is deep-seated in me.

Interestingly, I remember reading that Confucius, the father of Chinese bureaucracy, had constant trouble with bureaucracies wherever he tried to influence leaders. This is also true of Plato when he was invited to be with Pericles, the leader of Athens. Bureaucracy has historically created and managed systems to control all that live within its invisible walls.

This is not really a problem for most people since we are born into systems, such as the one called our family, and remain in various systems throughout our lives. Systems may be ubiquitous, so avoiding them may be impossible.

The creation of "systems" may be inevitable, and I suggest that bureaucracy may be necessary to serve the system and the people within it, but bureaucracy ought not to rule. I reacted against powers that sought to control me. Being responsible for my own actions was right for me. I have experienced and know that degrees of responsibility are what most people can handle. I also know that there are those who avoid any responsibilities. So be it. We need to recognize and accept the differences among people and respect what a person chooses for themself and how they live their own life.

Living under the control of professional administrators is what some people are born into. That is why I believe most people may not understand Prince Harry and Meghan's initial sense of helplessness. Prince Harry was born and raised within the royal bureaucracy. This is what he has experienced, and this is what he knows. He had expected that he and his wife would be cared for throughout their lives. After years of becoming accustomed to the structure and security provided by the system, it must have been a terrible shock to discover that they would be denied the care and controls they expected.

Although some of us would have it no other way, we must recognize that it takes courage to live one's own life and be fully responsible for oneself.

I am born helpless
In time I become able
Freedom to be me

If I am cared for
For how long and in what ways?
Knowing essential

Making Differences Work
09 July 2021

In many ways, we differ from each other. Sometimes our differences are glaring and may even threaten our own beliefs concerning religion, politics, or lifestyle. Or the differences may be minuscule, in which case we view what others say and do as insignificant behavior. In any event, we may prefer to be with people who have similar beliefs to our own. Yet, there is a benefit to seeking those whose ideations are different. My life has introduced me to a wide variety of people and beliefs, and I have grown and benefitted hugely from those differences. Without question, I prefer to be with people who are different from me. In fact, I owe much of what I am to them.

What makes differences work is respect for the individual, which must be mutual. The parties must be each themselves as opposed to reciting a script in an attempt to play a role they are not. Relative to this, I note that the more people I worked with, regardless of whether as a teacher or a leader, our respect for each other led to mutual growth.

This is particularly true when differences are authentic. That is when being oneself is not an act but real and powerful. As I have repeatedly said, the more authentic leaders are, the more their followers become real. Real means different—and differences are the most sincere gifts we give each other.

As a teacher, I taught people to be mentally present, understand what they heard, and be honest in response. Sharing thoughts and feelings as they are, not what one thinks the other wants to hear. When people candidly express their differences, it creates more opportunities for growth than mere silence or false agreements. In this way, our differences can become gifts.

We are not the same
But who wants to be the other?
Not either of us

We Are Products Of Our Past

05 April 2022

Now, as never before, my mind takes me back to the past. I look back on family, friends, and the extraordinary and powerful people I've been blessed to meet, live, and work with. I have fond memories of all our unforgettable kids and staff and those wonderful and exciting programs that blossomed from ideas into reality.

One member of my huge family, a former psychologist and professor at Berkeley, emailed me, pointing out that my growing up with eight family members in tight apartment quarters significantly impacted my child and youth programs. I agree, as I have a sense of my upbringing's considerable influence on me. Undoubtedly, it also shaped my work with adults about power, leadership, and the importance of dialogue between those significant to each other.

I believe this of all humans—that we become the product of those long-term relationships and experiences in our childhood and youth years. Those seeking weekend fixes and tools to become more than who they are might be under the impression that those solutions have changed them. It's only a start. Real change is a journey that happens over time. The most important thing is to seek growth while inviting and supporting others to do the same.

Besides long-term experiences, travel is another way to promote personal growth while expanding one's worldview. Watching people in different environments, experiencing other cultures and their achievements, and even sampling unusual and exotic foods are wonderful ways to accomplish this.

Lenette and I loved seeing and tasting the world and doing as much of this as we could. I believe we grew from it all, even during those occasional dangerous and challenging moments. So, what if you get lost? Eventually, you won't be.

Creating The Environment For Change

13 April 2022

Recently, I reflected on our multiple selves and that the best leaders nurture the better selves with whom they live and work. While recognizing both positive and negative human behavior, exceptional leaders create an environment that fosters positive relationships.

But, as I've written many times, if experiences that make up the past are especially powerful or repetitious, there is a strong likelihood that the past tenaciously remains part of our present. It does not diminish over time, but remains like a persistent itch that some can suffer without relief.

The rare, true leader never gives up on providing nurturing relationships and a supportive environment. Although they may be the salve that contributes to eliminating the itch from the past, the battle to be a better self is always one's own. Being open to growth and change is never easy. Erasing the past is impossible, but understanding it and setting it aside is not.

Yet, even the best leaders are unable to change another directly. They can only build relationships and provide an environment that is felt and seen as safe. Only then can others decide to change and grow. While never easy, given the right circumstances, it can happen.

There is beauty to all this. We can make ourselves into better humans. Still, we may not be able to do this by ourselves. History can be as tenacious as an octopus, wrapping its tentacles around us so tightly that escape seems impossible. Nevertheless, there is a path to growth and change. Help is there in the behavior of the quality leader.

Becoming Oneself

30 June 2022

Being individual and unique, and remaining so, is the job given to us at birth that continues to our death. I am that, and so are you, but not without help from our families and the world we will move into as we grow. I don't mean to suggest that without help and nurturing, we will not become ourselves. In fact, we are always ourselves, even if we hide behind our masks and personalities.

Pretending to be someone other than yourself is often attempted, but failure with those close to you is assured. Moreover, that failure will constantly come between you and your friends, acquaintances, and all those you work and live with. Living a lie is hell for all concerned.

Then why do people do this? It must begin early in our life. Parents and family are so influential that the marks inadvertently or deliberately made on our psyche are lifelong scars we carry, whether they are hidden or obvious.

Thankfully, help in becoming as fully oneself as possible exists. It is found in the relationships with those role models and leaders in your life. Ideally, this person is fully committed to you becoming you. They could be a teacher in school, a social friend, a leader at work, your mate, or perhaps a therapist you spend years with… And they'd have to be exceptional! I make the case that becoming as much oneself as possible is our lifetime journey, with every experience either contributing to or detracting from our being. Never give up the fight "to be."

Being Present
30 July 2022

I have recently written about "Being Present." Why? Perhaps it's my age, or I might simply be becoming wiser. What I have to say about presentness is a fact, not an opinion open for discussion.

Being present is a foundation that supports all else. If not present, you are in the past, the future, or unconscious. While the past is gone and can be retrieved if needed, it's still gone. The future is not ours to know. We can guess, calculate, and surmise, but we cannot see the future with any certainty. Even science and technology produce more questions than answers.

So, if my words carry weight, it's because the truth is truth. Now is where we all need to be. Why? So that we can hear and try to understand what is taking place or being said. The only way to confirm another is to have listened to them and worked to understand them.

Being present with another is what makes it possible to nurture relationships. It is the only way to create a "level" playing field where respect, regard, and even love can take place. Truth is hard, but necessary. If not present with another, both suffer.

Speak, I hear your words
Is this what you are saying?
To confirm a must

Creating Your "Better Self"

02 August 2022

A close friend invited me to write about becoming "A Better Self." I know this is doable for every human if they are willing to give time and energy to this pursuit and are lucky enough to have caregivers in their life.

The caregivers I refer to are people who feel good about themselves, have a sense of personal power, and possess regard and respect for every person they encounter. They give of themselves volitionally—not because of obligation or fees, but because they have a love for humanity and genuinely care about the people they live and work with.

A person who's aware of their troubled upbringing needs to know and believe that they are trapped by past experiences, but that it is possible to overcome them. It is also essential for them to realize that they cannot do this alone. Professionals, such as psychiatrists, psychologists, social workers, etc., may help. However, it is the caregiver I speak of who provides the best medicine for a conflicted human.

Is it wishful thinking that all troubled people can be made healthy? Certainly not. My twenty-five years of working with many troubled and challenging children and youth have given me experiential knowledge about this. I know because I am a caregiver and know what genuine caring brings to a person in need of this.

I am in deep pain
My self needs some loving help
Your love can help me

Can People Become More Than Who They Were?

06 August 2022

Can people become more than what they were and are? The answer is absolutely, with my usual "but." Emotional growth is impossible without relationships, particularly those that nurture. I speak of parents, family, friends, teachers, people we work with, and those who lead us.

The most effective of these is usually a parent or an older sibling who is close to us and takes us under their wing. Those who lead us also teach us "to be or not to be." In this regard, parents and siblings exert the most significant influence because they are there from our beginning. Being affected and shaped by them is at our roots. Clearly, we result from our family, but not entirely. And here is where change is not only possible—but likely.

How we take in our experiences, whether physical, emotional, or intellectual, creates the potential for change, even on our deepest primal levels. An example of this is our cat, Mia. About seven years ago, we rescued her from the animal shelter. When she arrived home with us, she was aloof and very protective of herself, scratching and biting whenever we got too close.

Slowly and carefully, we built a caring relationship with her. In time, there were no bites or scratches. Today, what she gives both of us is nothing but love and affection. She is completely part of our family. Also, at first, she never showed herself to others. Now, she introduces herself to most as part of whatever is taking place. "I belong" has become her message.

The same growth which can occur with our animals can and will happen with us with love and caring. When we listen and understand, the people we live and work with can and will likely change and grow. Nothing and no one is unchangeable. Love is that powerful a curative.

The People In Our Lives
16 October 2022

It all begins with two people creating another or more. Here is the unalterable fact that people need people. Why does this truth go so awry as we age? I wish I could answer this question to benefit those who find ways to alienate others. For everyone else, I offer how best to understand and nurture the most important relationships.

I make it my responsibility to build relationships, and it does not matter with whom. If a waiter in a restaurant, I'll build the bridge. If visiting a new doctor or any professional I need to see, I build the relationship. If it's the people that work for me or for whom I work, I build the relationship.

It is not that those I meet, regardless of the reason, are not intent on a relationship with me; I do not have any expectations that they will or are supposed to. Still, I do not wait. I desire to communicate with almost anyone I see as one of my own, which is me simply being a person. A smile, kind words, and "thank you" are so easy to do and speak. And why not?

When Barbra Streisand sings: "People Who Need People Are the Luckiest People in The World," she speaks to all of us. The words mean so much if we recognize how profound is our need for each other.

Never forget we do not exist except for others. Have we thanked them? Do we take the time to acknowledge those who have brought us into this world? Do we know their history? Have we taken the time to listen, understand, and appreciate that we are here because of them?

Sadly, I never took the time to sit my parents down and ask about their lives as children and young adults. Although I needed to know their story and family history, I failed to ask. It's a loss I can never make up for.

ON LEADERSHIP AND POWER

Leadership Basics
21 August 2022

I've written many papers on leadership. Yet, I feel compelled to write more. Of course, all I write expresses what I firmly believe, so agree or disagree; I'm fine—and you're fine.

To revisit: I often write that in 1975, when I first began to work with professionals and entrepreneurs, I was invited to help with staff problems. I was shocked when I discovered the leader was the problem—not their personnel. That revelation led me to become a serious student of leadership—which led me to the study of power. I read and took notes from every possible source: philosophy, psychology, history, and lots of Old and New Testament. Nothing was left on the table, even my own experiences. I needed to know what the great thinkers thought and wrote on the subjects. I do not have one, but I think I earned a doctorate ten times over.

I learned any leader could become a "good leader" regardless of past attributes, behavior, and life experiences. I also concluded that all the military academies and universities teaching leadership are blowing smoke if they only offer methods and techniques—such as how to look and say things differently. Teaching things that have nothing to do with good leadership is a waste of time. Exemplary leaders are not acting but "being," a behavior that is purely voluntary on their part.

Study and experience have given me the right to share my feelings and thoughts about leadership training programs. Leaders become outstanding because of their commitment to personal growth for themselves and those close to them—family, friends, and the people they work with.

This process demands that any leader venturing on this journey be moral, ethical, principled, and vulnerable. Vulnerability means they possess the courage to be as open with their emotions and thoughts as possible. If so, they set the example if this is what they want from those close to them. When it happens, genuine dialogue is made possible by the leader's behavior as seen, heard, and felt—and not by any other inducement.

Which brings us to another point—Who knows us the best? Who are the people that see us in as complete a way as possible? It's not ourselves, for sure. It is those we live with, our friends and associates. And most certainly, the inner circle at work—they all know their leader.

We are all known by others close to us so much better than we know ourselves. All leaders, without exception, are on stage with bright lights highlighting their flaws and strengths to these select few. Leaders are naked to their mates, children, subordinates, and all who are important to them.

How much better would our relationships be if we could be candid and vulnerable? Authenticity creates a level playing field. There is no pyramid, leader, subordinate, or child. There are only people sharing their thoughts and feelings. Is there a more powerful experience for people to have? Everyone involved benefits.

What makes leadership and all relationships work is trust, trust, and more trust. It is the most essential thing between you and those close to you. Then, how do you go about nurturing trust? Long story short, trust is not a two-way street until it becomes a well-established one-way street. It begins with the leader trusting and being perceived as such by those important to them—or else the seed isn't planted and won't grow. Trustworthiness must be reflected in words and deeds. As I have taught, genuine dialogue is not a matter of agreeing or disagreeing, but of the other feeling understood.

Establishing the roots for trust to exist and flourish is always the leader's responsibility. Relationships that foster honest growth require mutual and fulfilling authenticity. Regardless, leaders send all types of messages; not being mentally present, not listening, and therefore not understanding. There are other indicators as well, like a sneer or roaming eyes that tell staff they are wasting their time when trying to communicate with them.

How does it feel being related to in this manner? Might there be a payback? You can bet on it!

It is impossible to fool people with false words and behavior. Subordinates may comply for many reasons, but they'll never join in the trusting game if they're the only ones playing. Accordingly, some people enclose themselves in armor, and although they are assaulted and treated as pawns or less, they remain stoic and do what they must. For too many people, this means being as invisible as possible.

Certain indicators helped me to know whether change could happen with the leaders I worked with. I'll quickly revisit my discovery—one not found in any psychology or philosophy books: It wasn't the staff. It was the leader, in subtle or obvious ways, who was the problem they hired me to solve.

I've worked with leaders from almost every field and discipline, but before I accepted them as a client, I needed to ensure they had the courage to grow and to grow others. They had to agree to give me their power, not to lead but to teach—and they had to become one of the students at the table. In essence, they became one of the staff, and I related to them in the same way as I related to the others. The process proved that most leaders can become outstanding if they choose.

Who I am is not
I only think I know me
You may know my "me?"

The Best Kind Of Leadership

23 July 2010

What is the best kind of leadership? This is a tricky question because what is best for one type of follower will not work for another. Some believe they must be left alone to do whatever needs to be done. And, given the necessary space and resources to accomplish the job, they actually do better.

A good leader may discover that a person wants freedom but handles it poorly. Here, a good leader applies constraints like time, quality, quantity, etc., to either "grow or go" the follower. A good leader does this quickly, so that damage is minimized or growth is facilitated.

Inadequate leaders are too firm too quickly or too lax for too long. Timing has much to do with whether leadership is effective. Good leadership and teachable moments are as connected as ears on the head. Influential leaders mean what they say and do, creating no confusion between words and actions. The wiser employees know this to be true.

Better leaders also accept that differences are a good thing. Difference is desirable and needs to be nurtured both to benefit the individual and the group. Here is where quality leaders separate themselves from the not-so-capable ones. Growing individuals to be more competent, creative, and productive means also developing them as members of the group they work with. And by eliminating competition between those within and between groups, cooperation becomes the mantra spoken and felt by all.

Quality leaders are role models, students, and teachers. They are accessible, and they resource, facilitate, listen, and work hard to understand. They are consistent, firm, fair, and, most of all, accountable and responsible. When making decisions, they are made in the best interests of all involved, whether it be the individual, the group, or the client/customer.

Events Dictate

06 December 2010

I've said, "Events dictate the exercise of power" for over thirty years. Even if some might disagree, I know it to be true. One's response to those events can be too strong, too weak, or non-existent (doing nothing is still a response). Ideally, the appropriate response comes from the appropriate person, who may or may not be the actual leader.

When I speak of "events," I refer to those daily happenings that make our days unique from every other day. These can be the breakdown of communication, software and hardware failures, personality conflicts, and misinterpreted words.

The word "dictate" I intend to mean the demand that immediate action is warranted by one who can handle the associated issue. This requires some degree of "power" to take charge or designate another with the authority and resources to deal with the event at hand. It is at this point that many mistakes are made. Minor problems can quickly become large and unmanageable when events are ignored or not promptly addressed. Confusion or delays in matching the right person and the ideal response add another issue to whatever event requires the exercise of power.

When "things" happen to us as individuals, we can run, stand and fight, freeze, or embrace the challenge. Organizations have fewer options. Although events calling for an instant response don't happen often, most organizations lack a process to assess them properly. Only after disaster strikes do they become aware that a response is called for.

Exemplary leaders enable their people to act and exercise their power appropriately when called for without seeking permission from the hierarchy. Empowered by leadership, they can respond quickly and appropriately, exercising their power in ways that both save the day and grow their organization.

A Leader's Words And Behavior
10 June 2015

A leader's words and behavior are far more critical to those under and close to them than generally accepted and understood. Too often, leaders are unaware of their power to influence, whether through a subtle look or the actions they take. Those close to their leader are definitely more aware of who and what the leader is than the leader can possibly know. These individuals directly experience their leader's words and behavior and fully realize their impact on them. The leader is not blind to this but refuses to see themselves as the problem, typically blaming others for disappointing outcomes or negative results.

Those dependent on the leader, mainly those close to them, experience the benefits of quality leadership or the effects of destructive leadership firsthand. If the leader does not create the environment for authentic dialogue to take place, then mutuality is impossible. A safe space needs to exist between all in the organization, conveyed through words and consistent behavior that promotes respect.

Inadequate, out-of-touch, and destructive leaders are not cast in concrete. Their behavior was learned early in life, and what was learned can be unlearned. Any person who has difficulties in relationships—whether it is between two people or leading a classroom of students, employees, or a squad in battle—has the capacity to change, grow and know a different way of being. And by this, I do not mean or imply acting—that is a mere exterior experience.

The real challenge is a commitment by the leader to experience themselves through the eyes and words of those who know them best. This takes considerable courage from all involved. The others (subordinate to the leader) must feel secure and welcome to be authentic themselves—meaning they are listened to and confirmed by the leader.

Leaders must be genuinely vulnerable, open, and accepting, even if they disagree with what is being communicated. This kind of dialogue may not be possible without an appropriate facilitator or mentor, especially when attempting to overcome previous misuses of power. That is a difficult barrier to set aside. People may forgive, but do not forget.

Words alone won't bring a change in attitude, behavior, and understanding. Only the way the leader processes what they hear and feel will facilitate change. There is no nuance to this. A leader who chooses to grow never does this easily and without considerable fear. Not many people are willing to be vulnerable with those who know them best. This requires a change of perspective and understanding. True growth means rarely going back to where you have come from, but instead moving forward to where you want to be.

Who Invites Change?

22 July 2020

The other day, someone who had just finished reading my book approached me. He felt it dealt with leadership in ways he had not read in other books. He agreed that most problems in an organization result from poor leadership. But what he had to say intrigued me. According to him, I was communicating with two different groups at the same time.

He said, "On the one hand, you speak candidly to leaders about their power to influence through their words and actions. You confront the leader with their responsibilities and the importance of authenticity with their key people."

"But," he continued, "you also speak for the silent and disenfranchised majority—all of this often on the same page. However, you don't tell the subordinates what to do and how to communicate with troubled leadership. This is not a 'self-help book' for followers."

This is true. Only the leader can create an environment that invites genuine dialogue. If not, the followers will remain disenfranchised. Ignorance of one's power over others is no excuse. Acceptance and awareness of the gift that power is and using this power to empower those they have influence over is solely the leader's responsibility.

My book took years of work, study, and personal experiences. Like a good soup, it took time and ingredients to become a teachable philosophy. Those who have contributed to its creation know it is not about theoretical meanderings or wishful thinking. It is a practical guide to in-your-face, hands-on communication, and a path to genuine dialogue and mutuality. Many have told me that had they been aware of their power when running their own business, applying this leadership philosophy would, not could, have made an enormous difference in the success of their business.

Enlightened Leadership—Where Art Thou?

17 May 2017

For many years, I've written and lectured on leadership. I Have read thousands of pages on the subject and studied philosophers from different periods seeking answers to what makes a person an exemplary leader. What I've learned from my search, continuing to this day, is that an individual's life experiences and knowledge from those experiences directly influence their ability to lead.

Standing on the shoulders of great leaders who have come before isn't enough. Only through becoming muddied and bloodied are we able to become who we need to be. None are born leaders. In fact, there are no such people. Still, through experience, thought and action, trials and tribulations, a few outstanding leaders emerge. None are self-made but shaped through relationships with others—Regardless of whether their encounters were brief, accidental, or lifelong.

Quality leaders teach primarily by being who they are and, in the process, become students to those they teach. This relationship and its cross-influences are not necessarily formal but an organic way of relating. Sharing and growing in this manner are the natural processes that define "mutuality."

The trust leaders show is reflected by the knowledgeable people they invite into their inner circle. These remarkable individuals are not ideologues but those with considerable experience and success. They are proven leaders and are immune to manipulation.

The quality leader does not seek extensions of themselves nor waste time forcing agreement. This leader views each person as the unique being they are. Consequently, they engage with them in genuine dialogue and rely on truth, honesty, and fairness.

Jose Gasset, a Spanish philosopher in the 1920s, made the following observation to his students: "It is not easy to formulate the impression that our epoch has of itself; it believes itself more than all the rest, and at the same time feels that it is a beginning. What expression shall we find for it? Perhaps this one: superior to other times, inferior to itself. Strong, indeed, and at the same time uncertain of its destiny; proud of its strength and at the same time fearing it."

I quote Gasset because I strongly agree that the quality leader and "the leader as student" accept this as truth. Today is full of almost unlimited possibilities, and the leaders of this day and time are given responsibilities like none before. Now, leadership is becoming more critical than ever.

We might have once believed that we lived in separate lands and nations divided by natural and artificial borders that could stand alone. That assumption is now being challenged by increasingly limited resources, an exploding population, a degrading environment, and a planet that is growing smaller and smaller. These times desperately call for enlightened leadership. Hence the question: Where art thou?

Quality Leadership
27 March 2019

Saturday's *Wall St Journal* (3/23/19) has an article that clearly supports the message I've been trying to live and teach for seventy-plus years. It is about quality leadership as the key to success for the vast majority of organizations. That idea is nothing new. I am flabbergasted that this is the hot lesson of the day, which forces me to ask, what will it take for those in positions of power and influence to learn and apply so obvious a truth?

Since the beginning of group living, quality leadership has been necessary because it offers a better chance of survival. It has been essential to human creativity, productivity, and a better life for the majority.

In any successful operation that depends on people, there are outstanding leaders in the mix of what is taking place. Through their behavior, they become role models and mentors. Words may be part of their value to others, but their actions count the most. Yet, this is just the beginning.

The quality leader is not sitting in an office far removed from the playing field, but is a participating member without constantly being in charge. This point needs to be clearly understood. The leader I am writing about empowers those they work with to take leadership if and when the event calls for it. The ability to act decisively counts more than any fixed hierarchy or construct.

This is impossible to attain without trust, respect, and dialogue being established between the leader and their key people. These are the essential ingredients leaders bring to each of their meaningful relationships. As challenging as it may be, all of this begins with the leader being their authentic self.

How that authenticity is received by those who are being led depends on each of them and their personal history dealing with power issues. Whether they can grow and change has much to do with this. While nothing is assured, most people seek better than their past. They want to be trusted and respected and to experience dialogue that confirms their existence as a self. Quality leadership may not guarantee this, but there is no better way to reach another human being. Truth, respect, and openness have remarkable curative powers.

What is reported
It reads as if news today
Who cares? let it be

Leadership required
Someone must, without which way?
A leader at helm

Trust and true respect
What brings and holds together
Not easy to do

Dogs That Hunt And Dogs That Don't

05 March 2021

I know dogs, and I know people, and my knowledge of both is from lifelong experience. While I never studied dog behavior, my study of human behavior has never ceased.

The "Dogs That Hunt" take charge of problems and go off on their own to solve them without hesitation compared to those who don't or won't. What, if anything, can change a person's behavior so that they become a hunter? More importantly, do leaders benefit from that?

I believe that a group or organization with many hunters and too few non-hunters is headed for trouble. The hunters could potentially create a competitive and aggressive environment that may not contribute to an organization's growth. Also, a "sub-group" leader with power as their primary motive may emerge, working against the organization for their own benefit.

On the other hand, some hunters are assigned leaders and part of the organization's inner circle, and accepted as role models by others they work with. These talented people are prepared to take charge when the situation demands leadership. It is essential to acknowledge that they need the freedom to do what they do best when they take charge of the hunt.

Ideally, hunters and non-hunters must be committed to the principles of the organization and the primary leader. When that is the case, a few well-placed hunters are highly effective in reaching and going beyond an organization's goals. Maintaining a balance between the "dogs that hunt" and those that don't is vital to an organization's health.

I enjoy the hunt
Often the chase is enough
How freeing this is

The True Entrepreneur
11 October 2019

Good leadership is essential, but a true entrepreneur may be more important. What would our world be like without innovators and entrepreneurs who succeed at creating their vision? And where would any organization be without leadership leading people to succeed at what they gather for?

The true entrepreneur dreams about goals and how to achieve them. Rarely do they concern themselves with others beyond facilitating that. This single-mindedness may create serious relationship problems between people who live and work together.

Whether the true entrepreneur is focused on building a business for profit or securing funds for a charity, their approach is the same. Setting goals and working tenaciously towards them is what they do. The job remains the same, whether the entrepreneur's goal is finding donors to fund an organization or becoming wealthy. The challenge to achieve is what fires their creative juices, not how people feel toward them.

Because of the true entrepreneur's drive, their value to a group serving community needs can be tremendous because of their ability to win over donors and their determination to secure funding. If a volunteer group does not have an entrepreneur type amongst them, the wise thing to do may be to find one and bring them on board.

There is a reason for concern when adding a true entrepreneur to the group. Being goal-directed does not lend itself to caring, supportive relationships, and if they happen to be control-driven, a conflict between members is inevitable.

True entrepreneurs and good leaders are essential to society, although it is unlikely they are the same person. The tasks they have before them demand specific mindsets and behavior. Most entrepreneurs treat people as chess pieces. They are purposely not people driven. Good leaders are all about relationships between people and how they function.

How to deal with this problem is significant because the value of each to the group or organization, whether for profit or charity, may make or break it. The true entrepreneur creates the need for a group, and the good leader makes the group function properly and grow.

To deal with interpersonal problems that are sure to occur, a facilitator may be necessary. Genuine dialogue between all at the table is absolute. The facilitator's primary purpose is to teach and referee the rules of dialogue so that power, control, and manipulation by any one member won't rear its ugly head. As always, genuine dialogue is the key to a successful organization.

Entrepreneur, yes!
So necessary to us
They make what is not

Working With Volunteers
26 September 2019

Recently I've been working with a volunteer committee and have enjoyed the people and the process. But I've also discovered that having a mix of entrepreneurs in the group is essential. To be clear, the ones I refer to are entrepreneurial in the extreme. That is, their goals are far more important than other considerations. Achieving their ends is their focus, not their relationships with the people they work and/or live with.

When compared to true leaders, genuine entrepreneurs are entirely different people. The outstanding leader is about nurturing and growing relationships between people. They are at their roots, role models and teachers. Whereas the true entrepreneur is driven to realize their goals despite the cost to their relationships. Demanding that they be more humane in their dealings with others is akin to spitting in the wind.

Still, whether it be a for-profit business or a board of volunteers committed to community service, good leadership and committed entrepreneurship are necessary. This holds true, especially for volunteer organizations, for finding funding to sustain and grow programs is a significant challenge. Having true entrepreneurs in the mix to find and bring home the bacon neatly addresses this. Yet, entrepreneurs are not a good fit with volunteers who are committed to the good of the community. Most volunteers invariably care for the people with whom they contribute their time. Feelings, words, and behavior count a great deal. These aren't a part of the entrepreneur's playbook.

To be clear, I'm referring to winning entrepreneurs, not those who express their desire to be entrepreneurs but don't or won't exert the effort to make things happen. True entrepreneurs leave no stone unturned in their search to find and get the gold!

Entrepreneurs make things happen. They knock on doors, make the calls, and write the letters. They know exactly why they volunteer, and it's not about fuzzy feelings. Yet, they are often lousy leaders, not because they don't respect and work well with others, but because they are single-mindedly goal-directed. They step on toes and view the people they work with as a hindrance to achieving their foremost goal—filling the coffers. Volunteers still need to support the entrepreneurs amongst them, despite the possibility of conflict. Help them or get out of their way!

Working together
Takes effort, understanding
Do we give ourselves?

Some do or do not
So be a giver and help
Make it happen now

Do what is called for
Take necessary action
Maybe it will work?

More On Power

29 August 2020

Leaders are only who they are. That is unless they want to change and grow on a deeply personal level. If they have the courage to go there, they will need the help of a counselor or mentor, ideally, drawn from the people they live and work with. These are the people that know them best.

People with power too often believe they are fooling others with their words and behavior. They perceive themselves as winners in the relationship game. Yet, this is only appearance. They receive only a fraction of what their followers can give unless they are treated with respect, regard, and trust. Everyone loses if those conditions do not exist.

The belief that staff is what's wrong in the office brought me to the workshop circuit. Subsequently, my success with resolving staff issues resulted in many requests to help other professionals with the same problems.

I realized that by word and deed, leaders were damaging what they needed most to succeed in their businesses. If they wanted the best-trained staff and supportive relationships within their organization, something had to change. So, when we replaced monologue with dialogue, the results were impressive. Staff was empowered, and relationships and productivity improved dramatically. Going back became impossible.

Change does not happen in a vacuum and requires more than words. It needs to be seen, felt, and heard. Transformation includes the whole environment, including safety, trust, and mutuality. This is the experience of listening and understanding each other. The goal is to have employees experience equality and respect from their leader. Once this occurs, the elimination of a fixed hierarchy becomes a new and continuing reality.

Leadership And Role Model Workshops
06 November 2020

Providing workshops for people from literally every walk of life has blessed me with an array of tools and an understanding of what a successful education program in the "art of relationships" needs to be. Initially, I was employed to help professionals and entrepreneurs train their staff. Yet, I quickly saw that most problems with staff had little to do with them. The fault lay with the words and behavior of their leader.

This was troubling. Over many years as a leader, I had no idea that I may have been causing the problems I had with individuals who worked for me. I just took care of problems as they arose. Staff problems were always their problem.

My work with other leaders showed me the power these people possessed. I realized then that I needed to understand more about what leadership meant. I began an extensive study on the issues of power and influence over others. I read anything I could find from every source available to me on all related topics. My notes filled boxes stacked in my library from floor to ceiling. I became a true student—and loved every moment.

I also heard from leaders who sought me out, expecting to gather "tools" to better dominate and manipulate their staff. That they might be their own worst enemy never entered their minds or psyche. Self-growth was not what they sought, nor were they open to that. Ironically, many had years of therapy and still believed they were not the problem—others were the problem.

These people were looking to change their appearance, not themselves. It was always others whom they sought to change. I chose not to work with them. Instead, I worked with those who dared to accept that they might be the barrier to the experience they sought. The only real answers are genuine dialogue, genuine relationships, and unquestionable authenticity.

Workshop—Terms And Conditions

09 November 2020

My experiences have taught me that there are absolute conditions that must exist if participants in workshops are to benefit.

Most importantly: Being Present. How important is this as a beginning? Without being present, where is the student? People might be anywhere in their minds, but not in the workshop here and now. This is where they must be physically, mentally, and emotionally. If not, all is wasted regardless of the potential value to them.

For many, not being present is a learned response with its roots in unpleasant and even terrifying experiences. It could be parents arguing and screaming or subjecting them to physical abuse. So, early on, children learn to emotionally run and disappear. In essence, they learn how not to be present. As they feel helpless to respond otherwise, mental and emotional escape become the only option. It may even become their "go-to" when dealing with threatening situations or events out of their control.

Not being present in the "now" damages one's psychic and physical being. The scar tissue runs deep as it usually begins in childhood and continues to damage the person throughout their life. Even if safety is assured, being present is like walking on thin ice, with the option of retreat always at the ready should there be a need to escape. The present is where we need to live our lives. For too many, this is a rare experience.

Since I needed all participants to be as fully present as possible, I opened each new workshop by discussing the importance of this. If necessary, I would introduce a fun activity that would always show the value of being present to everyone, even those few who rarely were.

What follows in the next essay is the story of a process I've used where necessary. It's always a winner. I know this because people have taken it home with them.

An Experiment In Being Present

11 November 2020

When preparing the first workshop for a new organization, I tell everyone, including the leader and their inner circle, to come prepared to be as comfortable as possible. I suggest jeans or sweats because we might spend some time lying on the floor. Anything I can do to increase interest in what is coming has proven helpful, especially to people who have never met me.

At the first gathering, I brought a small boom box and a CD of Baroque music. I directed everyone to find a place on the floor and told them we were going to listen to about three minutes of Baroque music, adding that I would replay this same section of music four times.

The first time through, I wanted them to listen to the music as one entire picture. I played the CD, and people listened at different levels of attentiveness. A few may have been familiar with the music, but most were not. Regardless, they all heard the various instruments playing harmoniously with and against each other. Before playing it the second time, I asked them again to listen to the full Baroque orchestra.

After the second play, familiarity was quickly taking place. For the third listening, I asked them to select a single instrument and follow it for the entire piece, trying not to hear any other instruments. For the fourth time, I directed them to select the same instrument and filter out any other sound. At the conclusion of the fourth listening, I waited a few minutes and went from person to person, inviting their feelings and thoughts.

The experiences they shared were indeed powerful to them. At least four cried while sharing what they felt and, for some, what they saw. One told us of being visited by God and was assured that her mother would recover after a serious operation. Another said she pictured herself flying over the countryside, seeing colors and landscapes as never before. Each shared what, for them, was a remarkable moment during this experiment of being fully present.

The experience was a successful exercise for everyone. In future gatherings, we never needed to spend time discussing "being present." We all simply were—and yes, there was more music.

Without being in the here and now, we do not hear each other. If that's the case, we certainly can't understand each other, nor can we converse and feel confirmed relative to what we say and feel. There is a tremendous difference between hearing and listening. Dialogue with family, friends, co-workers and even strangers is potentially full of riches. Missing any of this is too great a loss. Consider what those workshop participants gained and learned about themselves through our simple music experiment.

I am here and now
A blessing to be present
Why be somewhere else?

The Key "Be Present"
Opens doors to know answers
Are you here and now?

Power, Failure And Knowing Oneself
15 February 2021

High demand forced me to seek additional help to work with organizations throughout the country. I needed someone with a deep understanding of my pragmatic philosophy about leadership, relationship, and dialogue. My own inner circle was the only place I could draw from since they each were fully immersed and understood our philosophy's intricacies.

There were three members in my Inner Circle who I thought would be up to the task. I approached one (I'll call him Joe) and offered him the opportunity to travel to organizations around the country and hold workshops mainly teaching dysfunctional leaders and their inner circles the art of genuine dialogue between them and their staff.

After I proposed this to him, Joe looked at me and said, "I can't do this. It's impossible for me to teach our philosophy to those with power."

I was shocked. What I offered him paid very well, far beyond what he was making at the time. Joe understood the philosophy and its application as well as I did and was one who never walked away from problems and challenges, regardless of how difficult they may have been.

"Why?" I asked.

His answer is of such value that I'm compelled to share it.

He said, "As you know, I served in the service in Washington D.C. as an officer and left because of the power structure I faced daily. I had many types of leaders, and almost all had no sense of their power and influence over those of us that worked for and with them. Their blindness or love of power eventually got to me and affected the work I had to do. I realized I needed to be in an environment that values respect and regard. Having experienced this with you before the service, I decided to return and was right to do so."

"But, while I understand and love our philosophy, I know if I lectured to leaders who were owned by their love for power and blind to the damage they caused their staff, It would affect me so negatively that I could not help them. I would fail, and failure has never been an acceptable option for me."

Knowing Joe and his background as I do, I understood his need to avoid failure. His complicated history and relationships beginning at "the kitchen table" remained potent forces in his life. For some, the ghosts of the past can never be overcome.

I understand the damage that power blindly or knowingly does to those dependent on the one in control. I also understand the good that those in power can do. My goal has always been to assist all involved in reaching a positive outcome.

Listening And Understanding
14 November 2020

When we're present, we hear what is being said to us. Yet, we may not understand or agree with what is being said. Speakers need to know that they are being listened to and understood so that agreement can possibly result. This is not typical of conversations between people who don't feel like equals. Here I could be referring to parent and child, teacher and student, boss and employee, or any relationship where hierarchy exists. These examples illustrate a speaker with the power to influence and a listener not having their true voice. These circumstances diminish the probability of an honest exchange between speaker and listener.

On the other hand, where and when genuine dialogues take place, people feel equal throughout the exchange. Here, the one with the power to influence empowers the other. Those feelings become part of the listener's experience. Now, listening and understanding have become part of the environment. In this event, the dialogue may lead to a real possibility of agreement.

The difference between dialogue and conversation is worlds apart. Typical talk or instructions from people with power directed at people who feel powerless is usually a waste of time. Feeling powerless is identical to being powerless. Those using power to dominate may believe they are heard, understood, and agreed with. Even so, expecting agreement is rare. Only compliance is likely, which is not what a true leader wants. People in power are responsible for building trust and empowering those they hold power over. How else can dialogue take place since it must be between equals?

In my workshops, I frequently stopped lecturing and, while looking directly at each participant, asked them to tell me what they heard, understood, and their feelings and thoughts. If they did not want to share, I thanked them and went on to the next person and asked the same questions. When someone spoke, I listened and confirmed what they said. I never asked anyone to agree with me. They shared their thoughts and feelings, and I listened. Over time, everyone talked—and interrupted too! Lecturing became dialogue.

Confirmation
20 November 2020

I use the term "confirm" to mean "I hear and understand you." The listener verbalizes their understanding, not by parroting the speaker but in their own words. They could begin with something like, "What you are saying is——," so if the feedback is in accord with the speaker's intentions, the speaker feels heard, understood, and confirmed. I also suggest that the listener's confirmation of the speaker and what they hear and understand nurtures the speaker to go deeper into their subject matter. What could be better?

I cannot over-emphasize the importance of confirmation to the speaker. Otherwise, how else does the speaker know the listener listens and understands? Any speaker of substance believes that they offer words and thoughts of value worth the listener's time and attention.

So what of the few who may appear to listen to the speaker but are mentally somewhere else? How is it possible for them and the speaker to connect? And, if not connected, what's the point of having the conversation, or of being a teacher, leader, or role model to them?

In the service, I held weekly gatherings discussing current news. I also taught elementary school pupils and trained a young staff at my camps how to work with children. In very little time, I discovered that many of my listeners did not always listen. So, like a professional comic dealing with a raucous audience, I developed an easy way of assuring my listeners were present. As I wrote in a recent paper, I frequently stopped talking and questioned my supposed listeners to tell me what they heard, thought, and felt about what I said. I asked for their opinions and invited dialogue, although at that time, my understanding of the significance of dialogue was years away.

From the speaker's viewpoint, checking on what people hear and understand is essential and needs to occur often. This is also a training device that, over time, brings even the most reticent to the conversation. Finally, if a speaker feels that what they have to say is important and necessary, they should take responsibility for getting their message across. Bringing listeners to the point of dialogue, questioning, agreement, or even disagreement is a gift.

I have this to say
All I ask, that you listen
Agree, disagree

Moving Towards Openness
18 December 2020

At first, I believed the main point behind my workshops was the information I shared with the participants. In time, I realized that what I had to say was not as important as how the audience felt towards me. Much had to do with what the leader who employed me told their staff to prepare for my first visit. Beyond that, what made the critical difference was the staff's personal perception of me. When I began my consulting work, I didn't understand this. Instead, I concentrated mainly on the material I presented. Thankfully, it did not take long for me to realize that to engage my audience, people needed to feel safe and that their comments were welcome.

I sought this knowing that the participation I hoped for would take time. Initially, only a few participants openly shared their thoughts and feelings without me pulling words from them. These few always seemed to have enough influence to bring others into the conversation. Also, I did not question why most people remained silent for as long as they did. As I have previously commented, this reluctance to express oneself begins as a child "around the kitchen table" and remains into adulthood.

Still, some would always risk being open and direct with their questions or observations. Dealing with feelings is essential, and I invited them to share what they felt. These few had no problem expressing their opinions and how they felt about issues I or others raised. Also, whenever possible, I clarified that agreement with what I said was not a condition of our dialogue.

Eventually, and certainly with the help of those who spoke freely, the non-communicators began to drop their guard and join in. Being open and sharing thoughts and feelings is difficult for many, but speaking out is a freeing experience. Everyone has something to say and contribute. In the right environment and given support, they will overcome their past issues and speak out. Occasionally, someone would say, "This is what I heard or read." I urged them to disregard that, as getting them to express what they felt was far more important. It is feelings that influence behavior.

Over the course of the workshops, individuals moved towards openness. Most found the courage to be themselves and to take on greater responsibilities. Yet, where progress was made, it was because of the leader's willingness to move away from traditional hierarchy and top-down communication to create environments that empowered others. Problems became much easier to solve when "my problem" became "our" problem.

Leaders who benefited from the training understood the weight of their power on their staff's behavior. They began to listen, understand, welcome candor, and actually enjoy dialogue with their team—perhaps for the first time. Monologues between boss and employee became dialogues between equals. The experience became fulfilling to where being at work meant being with family.

As family I belong
I am heard and mostly understood
I am me, you, you

Leadership—By Accident Or Design?

25 December 2020

The first principle of leadership is that leaders must accept responsibility for themselves and those they lead. Most people choose to become part of a group and accept that someone else leads them. There are many reasons, but generally, many do not want the responsibility of being in charge. So, accepting membership in a group and giving power to others is a choice. Arguably, most people take a follower's role because it's the easier choice.

Life plays games with us and accidentally places a few in responsible positions. If not by choice, they become leaders because others have chosen them, or their life choices made it necessary. A variety of examples abound: What is a parent sitting at the "kitchen table" with their children? A teacher in the classroom, a boss at work, the minister leading church services, or our influential friends? They are all leaders. Some have chosen that role. Others deny any desire on their part but are placed in the position.

Then, some simply love power. These include the dangerous and destructive leaders who seek needy and helpless people to use as willing pawns. They are driven to lead, as their love to wield power and influence over others is truly their aphrodisiac.

Hierarchies create different types of leaders. The hierarchy itself plays a significant role in the selection process, since they need participants who are willing to promote the hierarchy's message. In this instance, it's not a person that leads, but the organization's philosophy.

Regardless of type, leadership is a human absolute. Whether it is used for good or evil is always the leader's choice.

Designated Leaders

19 June 2021

The designated leader demonstrates through their achievements and attitude that they possess qualities that merit them a leadership role in their organization. How they go about doing their work and relating to others identifies their special qualities. Without exception, they are excellent workers and creative problem-solvers who do their job without making waves or drawing attention to themselves. They are responsible and accountable, but do not necessarily have an agenda that seeks a leadership position.

It is not uncommon for workers with exceptional talent and work behaviors to be considered for leadership positions. Still, the people I refer to are excellent employees with no expectations of becoming leaders. The differences between exceptional employees who do high-quality work (because it is their job) and those who seek to become leaders are considerable. Their intentions are different and eventually seen for what they are.

Those given leadership positions must also be trained to use their newfound power and influence. While the excellent employee will view this positively, it might prove difficult for the employee who wants and seeks that position. This is because their reasons and views regarding newfound power are vastly different.

For the outstanding employee, leadership is a job to be done as well as possible. The other who seeks leadership desires power over those they lead and likely is focused on themselves and their glory. What they do and how they lead are secondary. These differences are not subtle, nor are the outcomes.

It's Not About Tools

08 January 2021

My reason for continuing to write on leadership is simple. Without leaders, then what? Leaders are essential to existence itself, yet the responsibilities of being a leader are not well understood. Experience has shown me that most leaders believe that being an effective leader is about having and using the right management tools. In their view, the means for good leadership are easily employed, like a saw and hammer. Accordingly, they remain who they are—only the tools change, not them.

The leader who uses tools as weapons over others may win the fight but lose the battle. People know when they are being used and abused and will find ways to get even. The good leader knows tools are meaningless. They realize leading is about authentic behavior, communication, and relationships, knowing that what nurtures others will be reciprocated. What you see is what you get.

Good leaders are genuinely concerned about those they lead, relating to others as equals. They are relationship people focused on respect, regard, and dialogue, serving those they lead and empowering them to be as much themselves as possible.

This is a way of being that comes from deep within a person. I believe good leaders were nurtured as babies and children. In comparison, how were those that turned out to be poor leaders originally nurtured? The kitchen table is still where we receive our lessons on behavior. How different are we today as compared to our yesterday's?

It always comes down to this: our early lives are not incidental to who and what we become. Certainly, accidents and unusual experiences play a part in our being and becoming, but the kitchen table is one of our most powerful beginnings—we are only students of what others teach.

The Damage A Bad Leader Does

14 January 2021

Acknowledging the power leaders wield through their words and behavior is vitally important. Any leader that does not understand this damages themselves and those they lead. Instead of understanding themselves and learning from experience, they justify their positions and beliefs by blaming followers, events, and others for their problems. This leader must constantly defend their words and behavior.

This is foundational with most bad leaders and why they resist change. They want things to be what they envision and use their power to satisfy their expectations. The idea that they serve their followers never occurs to them. Instead, they demand being served. This leader expects certain attitudes and behavior from those they lead—compliance is victory to them. Again, this is a negative example of early lessons learned. People are not born this way.

The leader's words and behavior present those close to them with an accurate picture. They become the "king without clothes." Close followers know the difference between what is acting and what is real. Poor leaders only become real when they lose their cool.

Poor leaders do not seek the well-being of others, but only to satisfy their own needs. They require pawns to meet their demands, and the willing pawns know this. They comply because they draw power from the one they serve and exercise it on those below them in the hierarchy.

It comes down to learned behavior whether a person seeks power for the sake of power and self or uses it to empower others.

Defining Leadership

15 March 2022

One leader has recently inspired a flood of thoughts, which may lead to more papers on the subject. The leader I refer to is a seventy-one-year-old anthropologist who came to Camp Shasta as a very young boy. During the ensuing years, he has helped shape the world with his work and continues to be an extraordinary influence.

These days he lives in Berkeley and visits us frequently when he is not in Africa. During our visit last Saturday, our conversation drifted to the topic of leadership. He was adamant about not being a leader or ever having been one. I had to disagree. While in our memories, we saw no leadership behavior from him as a child and young adult, this is a role he has unquestionably assumed over the years. Beginning with his choice to further his education and earn his doctorate, he has since become a leader in every sense of the word.

When I told him this, he insisted he had never thought of himself as such. I replied that someone who gave all he could to others and enabled them to grow as individuals surely had attained the highest form of leadership I could imagine. He became silent as he realized I had accurately described him!

This exceptional man has grown into an inspirational leader and is the energy source behind the education of thousands of girls in Nigeria. His remarkable work and ability to gather funds and support for his programs are known worldwide. Events dictated, and he met the call. He never saw himself as a leader but as a "doer." Yet today, he is a leader on a scale most could never imagine.

The Inner Circle
27 March 2022

Not long ago, my ability and desire to write a brief essay did not exist. Today I have many thoughts, plenty of energy, and the will to act. I will let this paper be the outcome of just sitting at the computer. What will be will be.

My 35-year history of study and workshops with virtually every type of leader led me to write essays mainly on dialogue and authenticity. However, my extensive research on the history of power and leadership barely mentioned the importance of an inner circle. Because of one of my recent visitors, I realize there's much to say about the significance of the special people surrounding the leader.

My own organizations were blessed with a wonderful, high-functioning inner circle even back in the early fifties. I had no awareness of creating them, but I made it happen. Apparently, I felt this need and acted on it. My need for commitment and honest exchange between myself and a few select others was essential. While there were no issues about who held power, the people I trusted and worked closely with always expressed themselves as if in charge. They did not subordinate themselves any more than I did, and when the power to act fell into their hands, they used it appropriately.

The anthropologist I wrote about recently and his inner circle exemplify this. They have built and continue to build an organization that is changing the lives of thousands. Hopefully, other nations will replicate this model and make it even better. It could not have been accomplished by a leader alone, but by a leader and an empowered inner circle.

Power And The Inner Circle

24 April 2022

Leading others, whether as a parent, teacher, entrepreneur, or political or military leader, gives them the power to influence the behavior of those who follow and often upon whom they depend. Because of their position, contesting their power is often difficult, if not impossible. Yet, there is a way to moderate and influence the leader's behavior and actions. This is the responsibility of the inner circle.

Wise leaders surround themselves with a group of talented and courageous individuals. Still, when leaders create their inner circle, they must be willing to share their power and be ready to step up in their support. Inevitably, problems and issues will arise that must be dealt with at the moment. In those instances, the leader may be any group member in the best position to address the specific call. This ability makes the inner circle a vital gift to any family or organization.

Ideally, many members of inner circles can and will create inner circles of their own. To illustrate this point, usually most in the inner circle, although selected because they are superb employees, are employees—not entrepreneurs or professionals running their own businesses or enterprise. The actual leader and creator of the inner circle may also be an employee and likely a member of yet another inner circle. Regardless, all inner circles must be empowered by their respective leaders.

None of this would be possible without the building blocks I've written and taught about for years. Genuine dialogue and authenticity empower the inner circle members to assume leadership with the same authority as the true leader. Effective leaders know that when they entrust their inner circle, wisdom, not power, takes over.

The Root Of Failure
04 May 2022

A leader's behavior, especially their ability to engage in genuine dialogue, is always witnessed by subordinates. The best judges of this include family, those around the kitchen table, and those at work, school, and other relationships. So, it is always the leader, whether a parent or any person in that role, who, while talking, doing their job, or just being, can succeed in conveying an open, receptive and nurturing nature.

Yet, at the root of every leadership failure is a leader who only wants subordinates to follow them blindly. From that leader's perspective, they only desire pawns who will do their bidding instead of allowing followers to assert themselves. When this type of leader leads, the "truth" they get back might be what they want, not what they need. Often, this leads to disaster. When things go wrong, that type of leader blames others instead of accepting responsibility for their own failings.

Again, I emphasize that the core of relationship problems between leaders and followers lies in the leader's behavior, not the relationship. This failure is not a shared responsibility. How can it be when all the power resides in the hands of the leader?

There is no question that it takes a special person who will fill a leadership role with an open example of courage, honesty, and an authentic desire to help their followers grow so they can realize their potential.

I lead to improve
You, if you choose to be more
We help each other

Being A Leader

05 May 2022

There is no difference between being a leader and being thought of as one. Still, being thought of as a leader places that person in a position they may not have chosen. This happens when people volitionally elevate someone because of their attributes and behavior. In this case, people have selected a person to lead them who they trust to represent and protect them.

Otherwise, leaders are appointed by those in leadership positions. It's not the people they are to lead who choose, as this gives power to those not intended to have it. In most organizations, leadership selection takes place where a hierarchy exists. There, power and the methods of selecting leaders are well established and not easily shared.

The power to select a leader depends significantly on the type of organization. A sports team, for example, may choose a leader based on the contribution an individual makes to the benefit of the team and its members. A group of entrepreneurs may select someone to lead them for financial reasons. In situations like these, a quest for power is rarely a driving force, although it can exist. Knowing when and if power is the motive behind a potential leader's behavior is essential. It's not difficult to identify —only challenging to deal with.

I care for people
Help them as best as able
It is good this way

What Makes A Good Leader?

25 September 2022

My idea of a good leader is someone who is caring, nurturing, and an excellent listener. They also want and encourage people to be their own best selves. This leader knows that anyone who imitates another signifies weakness of character.

All good leaders are role models to those around them, influencing the behavior of others, including their inner circle. Not because they choose to be, but because they are authentic in all aspects.

Whether front and center or working behind the scenes, an outstanding leader's influence is everywhere. Water runs downhill, and a leader's influence ripples throughout any organization, large or small.

Wise leaders know their power, even if they believe it is hidden or invisible. They realize that encouraging or destructive words and behaviors exert a powerful force on every follower.

Organizations are like families, where behaviors are well known by those within. Faking authenticity is useless. Everyone will know if a leader is open, vulnerable, and honest. There is no higher calling for a leader than setting a positive example through their words and behavior while assisting others to become their own true selves.

If I lead, I teach
My influence telling too
I, a role model

Populism Is Not Leadership

22 October 2022

I consider a Populist "one who speaks to and for common people." This type of leader purports to know what the "common folk" are feeling, thinking, and saying. Usually, they voice this from the safety of their homes or while among friends. The populist leader is acutely aware of what specific groups want to hear if this aspiring leader is to generate followers.

A Populist, as I define it, is one who attempts to become this unstructured group's public voice. Despite what they insist, their goal is not to help the individuals in the group but to claim the power to represent them. In most cases, however, what the populist does and says is for their own advancement and self-aggrandizement. A populist cannot make a good leader if this last point is true.

Good leaders do not attempt to speak for any group. Instead, they seek to nurture the individuals who follow them to be as much themselves as possible. Their goal is to grow them into full participants and empower them to become leaders themselves. Also, good leaders do not lower their standards to the "common" level to seek popularity.

This leader realizes that they are responsible for creating an environment that facilitates and assists individuals who are unafraid to grow, and duplicate the same nurturing environment in their own inner circles. Respect, dialogue, and personal integrity are their hallmarks. Division and exclusion are the populist leader's stock in trade. Their power is exercised from the top down, with "divide and conquer" as their guiding principle.

When society is broken into "for and against," division occurs almost everywhere. When that happens, trust and dialogue become impossible. How can problems be solved when dialogue between people does not exist?

The outstanding leader seeks inclusion and the fullest participation possible between people of every persuasion. They unite their followers, increasing the opportunities for addressing problems and reaching a consensus.

ON PHILOSOPHY AND TEACHING

My Philosophy

18 July 2019

It was 1951 when Lenette approached my table at a UCLA job fair. She asked questions, and I asked questions, and in the process, I fell in love with her. Within minutes, I knew this was the girl I wanted to marry. She left the interview with a promise to return after canceling her job as a swimming instructor at the YMCA. During this time, she met two of her girlfriends and told them about me and the jobs I was looking to fill. She also mentioned, "His philosophy is awesome, and, by the way, he's the guy I'm going to marry." That's the truth!

I have never thought philosophically about my approach to working with children. I just did the best I could at all times and in all situations and wanted and demanded this of those I worked with. I would hold numerous training sessions discussing what apparently was my philosophy, but always emphasizing the pragmatic essentials. For sure, I was not theoretical in any sense that I was aware of, but "hands-on" practical. I was a carpenter, not a professor.

As an undergraduate and graduate student in my psych classes, I remember having issues with my professors over what was being taught and what I knew worked. My experience working with coworkers, parents, and children, always had a greater influence on me than what was taught in the classroom. As a practitioner in the field, I know my staff and I did an excellent job. Kids and parents were the recipients and the messengers. Also, and without question, staff and children ages four to sixteen played the most prominent role in what I became and my philosophy's evolution. The influence was never one way.

Years later, I was sought by professionals and entrepreneurs around the country to solve their problems with staff communication and behavior. While working to improve staff relationships and productivity, I discovered the real problem was the leader. This led to an intense study on anything and everything relative to leadership, power, and influence. It was then (in the '70s) I discovered that I did have a philosophy!

In general, my philosophy regarding any relationship is:

1. Respect the other, mentally be in the present, listen, work hard to understand, seek clarification if necessary and confirm what you thought you heard being said.
2. Agree or disagree, but honesty is essential.
3. Have the courage to be candid in response.
4. Be what you say and teach.

Who you see is me
Not an act to fool anyone
Good or bad just me

We need role models
We do not simply become
Experience counts

Bernard Palissy

24 April 2015

A family member sent me the following quote attributed to Bernard Palissy, a fourteenth-century artist, engineer, and writer.

"Even if I used a thousand reams of paper to write down all the accidents that have happened to me in learning this art, you must be assured that however good a brain you may have, you will still make a thousand mistakes, which cannot be learned from writing, and even if you had them in writing, you wouldn't believe them until the practice has given you a thousand afflictions."

There is an enormous difference between listening or reading about a topic and our total immersion in the same subject. It's why I stress the importance of our own experiences, whether planned or accidental.

While we must learn from what we do, we still must acknowledge the errors, omissions, and successes of others. Ultimately, that is how people arrive at that "aha" moment. It is where actual knowledge results from endless head, heart, and hands-on involvement.

How many times in a day do we hear someone say "I know" when they are merely parroting the words spoken and written by others? People say this even if they have not actually experienced what it is they say they know. In my opinion, they don't really know but only think they do. Too often, this means being closed off from genuine knowledge.

For thousands of years, people depended on pictures on cave walls, word of mouth, storytellers, and balladeers for information. The data instantly available today is almost overwhelming. But whether it be from a picture on a wall or the unlimited information on the internet, none of this can be compared to knowing from personal experience. Still, our personal experiences are never without bias, another factor complicating the issue of experiential knowing.

Have you ever played the game of "telephone" where someone whispers to the person next to them, and the next person repeats it softly to the next one, and so on, until all the people in the circle have the story relayed to them? It's comical how quickly the story changes from one person to the next. Do we only hear and see what we want to hear and see?

We humans are limited in our ability to be objective. As long as we have feelings and history, we also have influences playing on our thought processes and behavior. So nothing is crystal clear and pure regarding humans in their roles as reporters, storytellers, leaders, and teachers. Even if they have "been there and done that," the "knower" can never convey an exact truth. People are not cameras. Subjectivity is pervasive and is part of everyone's experience.

Being a student of other's written and spoken words does not lead to knowing, only a "between the ears" understanding. This is good but limited to answering questions, not solving problems. I firmly hold to the quote at the beginning of this essay. To really know something, one must experience it. The message is simple: Don't deny or resent your experiences—learn from them. To truly know, one must be experienced.

The Origins Of My Philosophy
24 August 2019

Where did my philosophy of living and working with people begin? I believe it all began in my family. My mom was giving, and although she had so few material things to offer, she gave love and shared all else. My dad labored through the depression doing his best to put food on the table; he was a hard worker, a strong union man, and never a blamer. While I never remember starving, I remember lots of soup.

My only sister was a queen, the second oldest, and very special to each of us, her five brothers. I was the second youngest. I only remember one bathroom wherever we lived, and we moved often. Tight living, competition, and tension between my brothers existed, but I was never involved in that. I honestly believe I did my best to be a bridge of peace between them. As I remember, they all liked me and treated me well. They were each very different, so learning about and living with uniqueness was what must have given me insight into the importance of differences. Space had to be respected and given.

Beginning early in elementary school, I was a member of a gang that stayed, played, and ran together until most of us left for the service. There was a very close relationship between us. Growing up in a Jewish ghetto made an impression on each of us. We all handled the experience differently. Some remained observant, and some didn't. I became a warrior, which meant fighting and defending anyone who could or would not protect themselves.

My only goal was to join the merchant marines and see the world. As I've written elsewhere, my experiences in the army played a huge role in changing my life, giving me direction and purpose. Change inevitably takes place when events and people are part of the action.

Having a philosophy means little unless you can live and share it, so I'll leave you with this: I discovered that being true to oneself, appreciating uniqueness, and learning from positive relationships made invaluable contributions to my life. If you can do this for yourself, you must want and do this for all others you meet along the way.

Self is not one's self
But a mix of many things
Life and living full

Life treats me so well
I must return what I can
Life decides not me

The "Problem Child"

02 November 2020

In the mid-fifties, I set up a counseling office in an elementary school. My reason for being there was to work with troubled students and teachers who felt they needed someone outside of the administration to talk to. One morning, the principal brought a young boy about nine years old to me because of the trouble he was causing in his class.

We sat looking at each other for a minute or two before I asked him, "What did you have for breakfast?"

Without hesitating, he answered, "I had Wheaties and a banana." I asked him who made his breakfast, and he proudly replied, "I did. I made it myself."

"Good for you!" I responded. "Do you have any sisters or brothers?" I asked.

"One," he answered. "She's seven, so I made her breakfast, too."

"That's great," I said. We waited another minute or two, and he asked if he could return to class. "Sure," I said, and he left to return to his classroom.

At lunch, about two hours later, I went to the teachers' lounge, and the boy's teacher literally ran over to me and almost breathlessly asked me, "What miracle took place when Tom was with you?"

"Oh, we talked about what he had for breakfast."

"Didn't he tell you about the fight his parents had?" She asked.

"No, it never came up."

"When he returned to the classroom, he apologized to me and his classmates. What happened?"

What had occurred between Tom and me that quickly erased his volatile behavior and transformed him into a positive force? Simple. I was fully present with him. He felt my respect and regard. I listened carefully to what he was saying and then confirmed what I heard him say. Also, my responses to him and what he felt assured him of a relationship of trust and mutuality. Finally, my candid response, "Sure!" when he asked to return to his class, nailed it all.

This was a genuine dialogue between equals, even if I stood feet taller than him and held all the power. Fear may have stood between us at the very beginning of our meeting, but our few minutes of silence and just looking at each other took that away. I have to believe that my look of acceptance eliminated any fear of me he may have had. Nothing but a little space stood between us. I intended this, and he experienced it.

What would have been gained had I conveyed my authority and power over him? Fear or even anger would have ruled his behavior. What might have resulted from that?

When I was first informed that the principal was bringing a troubled student to me, I immediately opened myself to anything that might take place, including a very frightened child. Most importantly, I made myself present. What better way to meet the unknown?

When his teacher came to me later, she was remarkably open to what I had to say. It was an instructive moment for her and the other teachers sitting around the table. I explained that making myself present and showing respect for him as a person set up the environment between and around us. It also had to be made clear that nothing I did was performance but was real—real to me and real to him. Anything less would have turned the environment toxic between us.

Tom's apology to his teacher and students suggested another possibility to me. I may have touched his "self." I believe our "self" loves and is the best of what we are. If true, he responded by being his best self.

The Classroom Environment
04 September 2020

Initially, the foundation and philosophy I built began in ignorance and blindness. I did what seemed the right thing to do simply because of events that called for a specific action. In time, I began understanding and developing a pragmatic philosophy that I could and did teach others.

Many years later, I started to work with adults, professionals, and entrepreneurs and to study power. This was when I began to seriously know myself. My formal education to understand people and behavior finally took off.

During the time I worked for the Los Angeles Board of Education in the 1950s, my teaching approach came almost totally from experiences drawn from my camp, working with children ages three to teens and staff. The formal education I received as a student at UCLA, as best I can remember, played little or no part in how I taught.

When I began taking over fifth- and sixth-grade classrooms, I clearly remember what we, over time, (teacher and students) achieved. It was a sense of acceptance, belonging, respect, regard, caring, support, and enjoyment of each other. It got to where weekends for the girls and boys got in the way of being at school with their friends. Someway somehow, we became a tribe—a community.

Even parents would observe and comment on the miraculous changes in their children. "What was going on at school?" became their question. Still, from a principal's viewpoint, it was quite different. They asked that I not discuss my classroom approach with other teachers during breaks. And to "please" keep my doors closed.

Academics never suffered. Reading, writing, math, science, history, geography, etc., were always front and center. Ah, but it was the "space in-between" that made the difference and brought out the humanity in each of us.

The Space Between
17 September 2020

In the last paragraph of the blog on the Classroom Environment, I referred to "the space between." So what do I mean by this?

Most people believe the teacher's primary job is to teach subject matter, beginning in pre-school through all grades. Covering everything and anything from art, dance, music, writing, reading, history, geography, math, and science, up to and including the most advanced and esoteric subjects. While they are essential, I don't think they are paramount. I believe and have acted on the premise that building respect and regard for each other comes first. Then, the subject matter becomes easier because help and participation occur naturally. It is vital to value each person as unique and that our differences are more important than our similarities. To make this come about is the job the teacher must undertake, making a total commitment to reflecting this through what they say and do.

This is "the space between," I refer to. It is, in fact, the primary space, and I argue, the most crucial space, where the teacher as a leader must be to teach. It is the place and time where the teacher's leadership and ability to be the role model must be perceived and appreciated by their students. That is the simple truth of our memorable teachers. They helped bring out the best of who and what we are. It is that time and space where teaching, leading, and being a role model are one and the same.

As our teacher, leader, and role model, this exceptional person has the power and influence to assist us in growing our potential and creating our desire to want this for all others. It cannot happen alone and all by ourselves. Ideally, it would be wonderful if this would take place around the kitchen table, but that doesn't happen often enough. Sadly, too much negative history is passed from parents to children, generation to generation.

Teachers As Leaders

22 September 2020

In the essay, "The Space Between," I wrote that preschool and grades first through third are when teachers have the greatest influence on affecting a child's behavior and worldview. The earlier a child is related to, the greater the opportunity for them to be influenced at their core. Thus, a teacher's potential to influence can extend into adulthood.

We must accept that the young child who comes to these beginning grades is already well formed by their parents and what takes place around the kitchen table. Regardless, the teacher still has an immense potential influence on the child. Here I'm not referring to the academics (reading, writing, numbers, etc.), but to their emotional, behavioral, and perceptual states of being. All are intertwined with one's sense of membership and connection to their peers and their leader—the teacher.

It's not about the academics the teacher teaches, but how the teacher leads. The teacher's behavior and attitude as a leader—more than their words—is no small thing. In my opinion, it's the most important message they convey and teach and how the influence they exude is magnified.

As the group leader, the teacher teaches what belonging and individual importance mean. Their behavior and words representing inclusion, respect, regard, listening, understanding, and participation all mix together, creating an environment that influences every child. Ideally, a feeling of self occurs, and each child experiences a change.

The leader-teacher need not set classroom boundaries because, with the student's participation, they are created and abided by. Support for each other is established, as is membership in a community. Each child is no longer a pawn to be lectured to or tethered by their adults. They know the difference, which is why weekends get in their way.

Philosophy At Work
11 October 2020

My experience with the Los Angeles Board of Education began in the mid-fifties and continued for a decade. During this time, I had counseling sessions with troubled students and teachers, performed inquiry training with fifth and sixth graders, and took over classroom teaching with challenging students. In addition, I did folksong concerts and was a "storyteller." My time with LA elementary school education was full, challenging, and fun.

My working philosophy came from my camp experiences with campers and staff. I made my students a big part of what we did in every possible way. In fact, dialogue was constant between us as a group and as individuals dealing with our unique issues. I was always available for one-on-one talks, and if they did not come to me, I went to them.

When it came to academics like math or reading, I would assign A and B students to work with a classmate who was a C or D student, while I would work one-on-one with failing students. When the slower students improved, and they always did, their mentor would be acknowledged and receive applause from their classmates. Also, it was assured by continually mixing them with each other that they got to know their fellow classmates and developed some degree of responsibility towards each other.

The relationships we established with each other were a constant. Nothing took place that did not accentuate both the student as an individual and the importance of the group. This grew to the point that Saturdays and Sundays actually got in the way of school and all being together during the week. The students missed each other, and perhaps they missed me being the adult among them.

In time, I realized I was a role model and not just a leader to campers, staff, and my students. While a role model differs vastly from being a leader, it is absolutely essential to a leader's success with those they lead.

Parents As Leaders

30 September 2020

It is a given that parents are leaders of newborn and young children. Parents hold life and death powers over their children and know they have little choice but to care for them for as long as they cannot care for themselves. Parents are also teachers, caregivers, and role models. Many, like myself, believe learning takes place before the baby is born.

There is no guarantee that the lessons taught are appropriate or desirable. This holds true for the most vulnerable periods of a human's life: Pre-birth, birth, and the first three to five years. This is so for obvious reasons, which all come down to a child's helplessness.

I've often used the word picture "around the kitchen table" because the influence parents exercise as teachers and role models is uncontested. The arrow points only from the parent(s) to the child. Extended family and others also add to the influences on a child's growth and development. This is why teachers significantly impact a child's view of themselves and the people around them.

The young can absorb incredible amounts of information quickly, especially social mores and how people relate to each other. This dynamic is as powerful as it gets. The young are vulnerable to other children and teachers in new, unfamiliar groups and environmental settings. Youthful behavior is not yet set, but continues to grow from these encounters. With age, vulnerability and openness diminish while the influence of learned behavior and attitudes grows stronger.

Under the influence of parents, the young do not choose role models. When introduced to others, including teachers and friends, they begin to select new role models. We, as a society, cannot afford to miss this opportunity. We must encourage and inspire young minds.

Ideal Role Models

25 October 2020

In every way imaginable, parents are the child's role models and, through the natural process, are connected emotionally, mentally, and physically to their creations. By taking care of themselves, the parents contribute to what hopefully becomes a healthy child who becomes essentially what their parents are.

I've extended the definition of the role model to include the people directly involved with the child until they leave the nest. During the first three years, the immediate family (mother, father, siblings) plays a vital part in whom and what the child becomes. I frequently refer to the symbolic kitchen table where most of the role model's power and influence are exercised, including all the home's permanent residents.

By the time the child leaves the nest, the child is generally formed and influenced, even if not fully conscious of the attributes and attitudes they carry with them. The kitchen table is a powerful teaching environment thanks to their role models; however, if the child sees this new world from only their kitchen table perspective, they are severely limited in what they know and believe.

Pre-school offers the potential for a whole new world and people experiences. Here, the relationships and the new and different role models will influence how the child experiences their immediate world, classmates, and adults. The opportunities are profound and must be taken advantage of. This is where the teacher is both leader and a role model. Teachers must have a worldview that respects and regards a child's uniqueness besides being able to listen, understand, empower, and care for them. The teacher accepts and uses subject matter as only a part of the education experience and understands relationships and dialogue count for so much more. The ideal role model knows we are each more than a self—we are family.

Being Is Not An Act

03 December 2020

Even compared to the child's home and early indoctrination and education via parents, early grade teachers are given tremendous power to influence a child's attitude and behavior. This may be positive or negative, and why it is essential that teachers understand and accept this.

Teaching a subject like reading and math is one thing, but being an exemplary leader and role model is an entirely different competency. This is no scripted role, costume, or act—They are authentic in every regard.

As I have written repeatedly, quality leaders lead by being present; they hear what is being said, do their best to understand what is being said, and seek clarity when necessary. They confirm the speaker, letting them know they are heard and understood.

Leaders want dialogue between equals and do not seek false agreement. Quality teachers are leaders who want to understand. They willingly set aside their power and influence to positively empower others. If growth and empowerment are what the teacher wants from their classroom, they will be genuine in their efforts to provide this. Their openness and receptivity will be felt by all.

Those who value power over others cannot hide their true intentions, and no one is fooled. Playing to the will of those who love and abuse power is a game everyone loses, including the leader who lulls themselves into believing they win. No one wins in the game of power.

I want you to "be."
Not me, but to be just you
We are now double

What Can We Learn From Lecture?

27 April 2021

During a lecture, we see, and we hear. It is likely that some understanding of what is seen and heard occurs. But without an invitation and opportunity for spontaneity between presenter and student, how is the audience to ask questions, make comments, or express an opinion? If the chance to interact when needed is denied, what and who is being served? Might this be felt as abusive by those who may already have issues with inappropriately used power? How can this lack of interaction facilitate relationships, and how can any teacher see this as unimportant?

Learning from a knowledgeable teacher is a gift and, ideally, where dialogue happens. Too many teachers are unaware that their power must be exercised as a beneficial source in their roles as moderators, teachers, and presenters. Deferring a student's ability to ask questions or comment when they need to be made is the worst possible teaching situation I can imagine.

Consider that when teachers and students pay genuine attention to each other, respect exists in the space between them. They become equals in the give and take of the moment. They listen, seek to understand, and are candid in response. The result is learning or the best opportunity to learn, which becomes the teacher's finest gift to the student.

Students have little opportunity to learn in an environment that limits itself to presentation alone. A lecture rarely allows questions, comments, or opinions until a specific time. In a teaching environment, this can only restrict the learning potential. Students experience this restriction and the thoughts and feelings that come with it. Will a learning experience of this type help us become more ourselves and more of an individual contributor? I think the answer is obvious.

Training Potential Leaders
22 March 2022

Military schools and universities with leadership programs have the right idea, but they need to clarify that no classroom instruction makes leaders. All they can do is teach methods. And while that may have some value, methods themselves have very little to do with being a quality leader.

Personal and constant experience is the foundation of good leadership. Judgment and knowledge are gleaned from many events, beginning in our childhood. One example is the child who grows up in a family that assists and supports them in being responsible for themselves and others. The child models that behavior not by being told, but by experiencing this from those closest to them. The experience of being a full member of the familial group and being heard and understood is what makes a child hear and understand.

We are what we learn
What we learn may not be true
How do we find truth?

I am me, you, you
That is the best it can be
We each must be self

I need a leader
Not to lead me, but show me
We care for each other

Socrates, Aristotle, And Plato

04 September 2022

Socrates believed in the individual, and that true power exists in people being themselves. It is why the dialogues with his students remain so meaningful even today. He pushed each of his students to find and be open with their feelings and thoughts.

Aristotle believed that democracy, as a collection of individuals, was, among other things, the best path to governance. Plato disagreed, believing that democracy would eventually lead to weak leaders and create opportunities for a strong leader, or dictator, to take over governing.

Of the three, I consider Socrates's point of view best and most relevant to my own beliefs. What I wanted from every individual I taught or worked with was they should be as much themselves as possible. A leader's job is to help bring this about as an example and mentor.

The study of power and leadership is something that nations, corporations, professionals, classroom teachers, and parents must bring to their inner circles and the kitchen table. A leader cannot be less than what they hope for from others. While this is easy to write and talk about, it is challenging to do and be.

Power in our hands
Use it as love and learning
We all benefit

Recognize myself
My need to know and to grow
It is why I ask

Do not back off you
Express what is inside you
Be you not another

ON GENUINE DIALOGUE

Rules Of Engagement
14 May 2021

There is a vast difference between what most of us consider dialogue and what I call genuine dialogue. Conversation between most people is loose and without fixed and agreed-upon rules, so it can often end up feeling that there was little benefit to the time spent talking and listening to each other.

Genuine dialogue has rules like those essential to sports. What would baseball, football, basketball, etc., be like if the rules were loose or non-existent? The game would not exist. Rules make the difference between having a conversation or experiencing genuine dialogue.

Here are the rules that make genuine dialogue work:

1. The participants must be mentally present with each other.
2. They must respect each other and listen to what is being said—instead of building an argument against what they think they've heard.
3. Finally, to ensure that the speaker knows they have been heard and understood, the listener needs to repeat in one's own words what the speaker has said. For example: "So what you are saying is—. "

If these rules are followed, the listener feels safe and can be candid with their response. What makes this work is the acceptance of the listener and the speaker that agreement is not asked for.

If the speaker or listener expects agreement to result, they must lay their expectations on the table at the beginning. Compare this to most of our conversations with others. We enter them fully expecting agreement or that our position is the correct one.

When I began working with leaders throughout the country, they initially employed me to speak to the issues of staff and leader relationships. The leader viewed the problem as lying solely with the staff and their relationships with each other. Instead, I found the root of the problem was the leader's communication style. This exercise of power was not invisible to their staff or me.

I developed the rules for genuine dialogue techniques to build a platform for better communication skills. That way, everyone wins the game.

Technology vs. Genuine Dialogue

13 February 2011

I may be the wrong one to attempt an essay on the joys, hopes, rewards, and potential of technology, let alone its myriad problems. I want to learn how to use and benefit from this remarkable phenomenon while, at the same time, not having it replace the "face-to-face" dialogue I have made my lifelong work trying to understand, use and teach.

My first thoughts are that communication between people is not the problem. We are probably more in touch with each other than at any time in human history. But what is now considered "being in touch" is like walking over water instead of swimming in it. That is, we communicate with each other but without getting ourselves wet. Meaningful face-to-face dialogue is all about getting wet! And genuine dialogue is like having a spiritual, full immersion experience.

Our technology facilitates a communication experience that is not only dry but antiseptic. What we touch is not each other, but a tool. Too few are immersed in significant relationships that require, even demand, a sharing of space separated by a few feet and often inches. In person, eye-to-eye contact gives us a full-bodied message compared to only hearing and seeing words. How can this be accomplished with small handheld objects or computers?

If we are to hold on to our humanity and the primary purpose of our being, it must be through our relationships. We need to move toward being there for each other, hearing and understanding each other, respecting our individual differences, and—yes, loving our neighbors as we also need to be loved. We must be present when we meet face to face, or how else do we confirm each other?

Some say that if one can count five friends in a lifetime, they will have lived a rich and full life. We may call the multitudes we reach on Twitter, Facebook, or E-mail our friends, but I don't think so. And, I venture, neither do you.

Put aside all the technology you are using as often as possible and begin anew with your truly select friends. When with each other, be mentally present, and show respect for the uniqueness each brings to the table. Listen and confirm what is being said without expecting agreement. Express your truth and let them do the same without judgment. Finally, look into the other's eyes as they look into yours. Now you've experienced genuine dialogue.

The amount, speed, and data transferred between people over enormous distances are not simply remarkable, but are reshaping our world. There is no nation, business, community, religious institution, or family that is not experiencing the effect of this technological revolution. We as a society are just beginning to understand where it may take us, and in many ways, we are unprepared. Information is influence, and influence is power. The potential for great good or evil now travels at the speed of light.

Communication Is The Problem

02 August 2011

The stuff that happens in Washington, D.C., is absolute confirmation that communication is the problem. In the business world, whenever decisions need to be made, they are made. They may not be good ones, or they may be slow in coming or arrived at too hastily—even so, they are made. It's the leader's responsibility to get what needs to be done, done.

Businesses are not democracies, and the leader is not an elected politician whose primary purpose is to represent their constituents. So comparing political leadership to business leadership is as foolish as comparing the operation of a government with that of a business.

The political leader has many strings attached to what powers they appear to have. They fear their power may be withdrawn if the constituents' needs go unmet. The business leader "owns" both the power and the strings. They fear the loss of money and business, but not the voice and vote of their employees.

Politicians worry too much about the voice and vote of their constituents to the loss of the "greater good." Similarly, the business leader does not understand how important the voices and votes of their employees are to their business' success. The former is weakened by knowing they have too little power, and the other by believing they have all the power. Neither is true.

Aside from the differences I pointed out earlier, leadership in politics and business share a significant commonality. Both need the support of the people they lead. Those who voted the politician into office and those who work for the business leader.

Yet, if the politician is to move beyond the constraints of their constituents to the larger and more essential needs of the country, they must mentor their constituents to this "greater good." This is never easy, but essential if democracy is to work. The alternative can only fracture a democratic country into hundreds of isolated and weakened camps.

Similarly, business leaders need their people to support them as well. But this is a challenge beyond what most understand and, therefore, are incapable of achieving. Getting employees to a committed level of performance beyond earning a paycheck is every bit as difficult as teaching one's constituents to understand and support the "greater good." Neither is an impossible task, but both require courage to communicate genuinely, patiently, and clearly.

All the work my team and I did together over the years was aimed at helping leaders facilitate communication and problem-solving authentically. Genuine dialogue was taught so that honest opinions could be brought to the table for the good of the whole.

For every politician and business leader, communication is the problem. Since what and how they communicate is experienced by each individual they influence, what people perceive ends up as one's own truth, even if not necessarily what is actually said or done.

Hence, if the issue for a country is the greater good and the issue for a business is success and growth, both types of leaders need to be authentic in what they say and do. For the politician and the business executive, this means a knowledge of the subjects, the ability to negotiate, understand the other, explain, enlighten, learn, and the willingness to give a little to get a little. Although they face different issues, the challenge for both is the same: authentic and effective communication. In other words, genuine dialogue.

Dialogue
15 February 2020

When I write, my own thoughts take precedence over what others might think, although I try to be open to what others have to say. I really want and value dialogue, so when people comment, pro or con, and transform the monologue into dialogue, it's like catching a fish—the entire point of casting my lines. It's what I look forward to, regardless of whether we agree.

I frequently express my feelings and thoughts about relationships, communication, dialogue, power, and leadership. These are the subjects I have read about, researched, experienced, and taught over the years. They are also the primary building blocks I used to form my philosophy. I freely admit to changing the theories of others, but if they proved impractical to me and those I worked with, I discarded them and created my own. Whatever I used and taught had to be practical and work.

Still, my personal experiences have been and continue to be my primary mentor. I am thankful for them all, including the bad and painful ones. They each taught me something of value. I remain a continuing student of what life has to teach me, so the learning continues. Getting older is teaching me stuff every day.

Dialogue is best
My thoughts are made known to all
How good can it be?

Free Speech, Facts And Opinion

19 February 2021

A dear friend sent me a book that he believes makes the case that "free speech" is fighting for its life in our country. It's written by a conservative professor and details his frustration about being able to express his opinion on various issues. He contends that freedom of speech is denied him and others like him. The professor also argues that he is unable to express "truths" by the institution where he teaches. He asserts that universities throughout the country are responsible for shutting down free speech in the classroom.

I agree with him with being able to express one's opinion. That's what "genuine dialogue" is all about. People are mentally present, work to understand what is said, and are totally honest in their responses. Agreement either happens or does not, which is acceptable. The question then becomes, are facts necessary in most conversations, or do opinions rule?

The professor's argument overlooks the reality that when influential people speak, their words are often taken as fact. Unless facts are backed up by provable data instead of the power and influence of the speaker, how can we know what is said is true? Some people believe every word uttered by those with influence or impressive credentials, accepting every assertion as fact, without any need for proof.

Opinions are what most people share and are commonly based on what one has heard or read. Personal prejudices are also a factor. Knowing the difference between what is fact and what is opinion is essential to almost every conversation we have with each other.

Free speech is just that. One can say anything they please, leaving it up to the listener to separate fact from opinion. Facts are irrefutable, but opinions are always arguable. In academia, there is room for both if the speaker is clear about which is which.

Fact, Fiction, Opinion, And Expectation
28 February 2021

The differences between each of the title words are significant and complex. If I personally experience an event, this becomes a fact to me because of my participation. "I was physically there. I saw and heard firsthand." Still, if I express what I think and feel but have not experienced an event, I can express only my opinion.

Fiction is false, a made-up story, often crafted to mimic truth and fact. Knowing the difference and responding appropriately to fact, opinion, or fiction is never easy. Seeking concrete data to support what is said and heard is not a simple process. One must search for hard proof. Merely saying it is so does not make it so.

Examples abound around most "kitchen tables," where much talk takes place and where separating fact, fiction, and opinion is often next to impossible. That is why I include the word "expectation" in the title. Expectation is usually below the surface, but it plays a significant role in communication. Often the expectation is that "I'll win you over to what I say because it's true." Here is where opinion and fiction become one. Spinning fiction into fact and having the listener accept it as such is the speaker's goal.

The genuine dialogue experience may be the only way we can communicate with each other if a speaker believes strongly in what they say, even if they are repeating what they have heard or read. What many people believe is true is based on sources that assure them "What I say is actual." Today, this kind of communication has become more common than ever due to technology and social media that convincingly makes fiction appear as fact.

It used to be that most people communicated their opinion to each other, and they would say so, but this is becoming rare between us. It is why I suggest asking questions like these:

Is this your experience?

Were you there?

If it was what you heard, how reliable is your source?

We must put aside our expectations that what we are told is accurately represented. Fact demands irrefutable proof, and we are each responsible for separating fact from fiction. This mountain is getting harder to climb.

Our world is changing
Must we also change with it?
Maybe, maybe not

Emotional vs. Rational Thought

18 May 2021

Genuine dialogue, while desirable, must be carefully and thoughtfully entered into. While I wish for genuine dialogue with those important to me, it may not always be possible. The experience requires committed participants who understand and live by its rules.

Depending on the subject, genuine dialogue may be challenging to undertake. The current political climate is one example of how complex and difficult this can be. The beliefs and powerful emotions of the conversationalists may discourage any give and take in the head and heart of the communicators. In such instances, positions are so firmly established that genuine dialogue can be nearly impossible to invite and enjoy.

The process of being present and open to understanding the other's words and beliefs, and assuring them you've heard and understood them, is a must before expressing one's own position. And, when ideations are strongly ingrained, this is difficult to do.

Research and brain theory suggest that the amygdala developed earlier than the neocortex. This part of the brain controls our emotional outbursts and the physical actions that follow, considered an early survival mechanism. In contrast, the neocortex, which comes later in our evolution, is a higher-order, fact-based brain function that influences our behavior, moderating our emotional reactions.

So, does our inability to engage in certain subjects have more to do with the biological sources of influence? In this regard, are we more like our ancient selves, allowing powerful emotions to influence our behavior? Or do we allow ourselves to be influenced by a fact-based reality and rational thought?

These are interesting and serious questions every individual needs to ask and know about themselves. Not surprisingly, those with whom they live and work closely will likely know the answers. They are those who know us best.

Like Family
28 June 2022

Sharing a dialogue with someone I have been close to for seventy-plus years is always a wonderful experience. I'm lucky to have this opportunity with many. While agreement is the more common experience when having a conversation, now and then disagreement can also result, which is also a good thing. It's worth remembering that agreement has little to do with the beauty of dialogue.

I've employed genuine dialogue throughout my relationships with people, even before I understood its importance to me and those I communicated with. When I eventually defined the rules and fully realized its significance, I knew it was a game changer in every way imaginable.

Genuine dialogue levels the playing field with whomever it takes place. It is the way for those in power to share their power by effectively communicating, even when they disagree, which is of considerable importance.

I'm experiencing the value of this last point now with someone I consider family. He was a child when he came to me in the fifties, and I am proud of his achievements over the years. Yet, we hold vastly different political, social, and economic views. Nevertheless, our ability to engage authentically with each other is something we both value dearly. We may disagree, but we continue caring for each other as family with love.

ANIMAL STORIES

Our Beloved Animals

06 August 2021

Animals have been an important and fulfilling part of our lives. I'm sure this is also true for many of you, so sharing a few experiences with our animals might bring back memories of your own.

After Lenette and I were married, we had three animals. Brutus was our first, a brown and black Beagle who entertained us with his math expertise and other antics. While sitting up in my arms looking like Charley McCarthy, he—so help me—this is the truth, responded to my questions with barks. If I asked him the answer to two times three, he barked six times. Two from four, two times, and so on. He could count, multiply, divide, and subtract numbers. I swear I gave him no help whatsoever. He somehow just knew.

Brutus's best friend was our huge German shepherd, Heidi. She was a puppy brought over from Germany and given to us as a gift. She grew into a remarkable protector of our family, which, of course, included Brutus and Cleo. Cleo was a pure white cat who, in her lifetime, managed to have a total of 48 kittens!

Whenever Cleo gave birth, Heidi would stick her head in the birthing box and pick up each kitten almost as if to swallow them. Then she'd take them and clean them thoroughly before returning them to their mother. Clearly, the three animals cared for each other.

At dinner, Cleo would play games with Heidi's bowl and food. Many evenings we would watch her attempt to take over Heidi's food bowl by slowly pulling it towards her. After each relatively successful move, Heidi would move closer to Cleo until they were a head apart. This continued until Heidi's bowl came within range of Cleo's mouth. At this point, Heidi would let out a warning growl, curl her upper lip, and display a canine. Only then did Cleo withdraw to a safe distance. Regardless of the games they played, they loved each other.

Lizzy
09 August 2021

I have many "dog stories" to tell, and I'll try to share them in the next few essays. This is the story of Lizzy, an Otter hound and one of the most unusual members of our family of animals. Lizzy was unlike any animal we've ever had. Otter hounds are a rare breed, about the size of a German shepherd. They are slim, fast, and lovers of water. Lizzy's unique feature was her fur, which stuck out in a wild and independent way—which she most certainly was.

She had her own ideas about almost everything and showed those independent characteristics whenever we went out into the wilderness to play and hike. Besides Lizzy, our animals at this time also included Toulouse Lautrec, a Basset hound about as close to the ground as a dog could get, Bear, a big and gentle Mt. Pyrenees, and two cats that fancied themselves as dogs.

During this period, we lived in the country south of Reno with almost nothing around but sage. To the west was Mt. Rose and a ski area known as Slide Mountain. The three dogs and two cats spent much of their day outside in this country. Yes, the cats went with the dogs almost everywhere, keeping close to them regardless of where they roamed. Together they spent hours in the fields, often returning home as the sun set. At first, it was Bear that they followed, but as Lizzy grew, her breeding took over, and she became the group leader. Being a full-blood Otter hound, her history was being part of a group, and that's what she demanded of the other animals. They were her group, and all followed her.

Lizzy seemed to always know where she was. One day, we went into a meadow of deep snow, and the animals went crazy with joy. They loved the snow and ran wild for hours until exhausted before they followed us as we cross-country skied. They did, but on this occasion, Lizzy did not. She took off for the nearby hills. Some time passed, and we gathered up the animals for our trip home. Yet, Lizzy hadn't returned, and we didn't know where she had gone. We called to no avail. Nor we did not see her, but she saw us and played her game of independence. We had no choice but to start the motor and act like we were heading home. It was getting dark. But Lizzy saw it all and understood she'd better join us or be left behind.

Then, out of the darkness, Lizzy appeared with a look as if to ask, "What about me?"

That was typical Lizzy, and we all left for home.

Call Of The Wild
22 July 2022

During our first summer at Camp Shasta, we used our neighbor's lake to teach swimming and enjoy. The neighbor who allowed us to use his lake was also the man who sold us the land for the camp. Carl Parks was a successful logger and a professional bear and mountain lion hunter. He had a large Alaskan husky that he would take on his hunting expeditions. Whenever this dog broke free of his leash, he hunted the dogs of his few neighbors. It was a serious problem. Carl's husky killed several dogs, which our neighbor paid dearly for. So he kept the husky chained because he realized those who lost their dogs would shoot it on sight.

In the spring, before we opened the first year of camp, Lenette, myself, our German shepherd Heidi, and our beagle, Brutus, decided to hike down to Richardson Creek—our property line to the north. We constantly walked our forested land so we could be as familiar as possible with it all. On this day, I brought a large machete with me.

The forest was dark and beautiful, and our walk was enjoyable. The dogs ran in all directions, checking out every rock and tree. But a real danger was lurking in wait. I saw the husky crouched in the forest, so I grabbed Brutus. In that same instant, the husky leaped and tore the small beagle from my arms. I picked up my fallen machete and hit the dog with the flat side of the blade. It bounced off him and flew ten feet away from me.

I looked for a rock or piece of wood to get the husky to drop Brutus, who was hanging from his jaws. Heidi rushed the attacker from the side, striking him so hard that he released Brutus. I grabbed Brutus, who was like a limp rag in my hands. I thought he was dead and looked at what was now happening in front of Lenette and me.

The two dogs circled each other, instantly bringing to mind the battle between Buck and the wolf pack leader in "Call of the

Wild." That was fiction, but this was real, and life or death was intended for one or the other of these two magnificent animals. There wasn't anything I could do at the moment. It wasn't possible to get between them or try to hit the husky with a rock or something. All we could do was watch.

The husky lunged at Heidi, but she evaded his forward rush and instantly went for his neck. She lifted him, gripping his neck in her jaws, and in a single motion, threw him to the ground. It was obvious she was in this fight to kill or be killed. Fearing the worst, I grabbed Heidi's tail and screamed at her to let go. She hesitated and glanced at me as if to say, "Are you sure?" before finally releasing him.

The defeated husky remained on his back, feet in the air. He had given up. We watched as he slowly turned on his stomach and, just as slowly, crawled back into the forest. Heidi watched until the dog was entirely out of sight, alert for any aggressive move. She turned to Brutus, who I was still holding, and licked him. Brutus leaped from my arms and began kissing Heidi in pure joy, as if knowing she had saved his life. They continued chasing each other around, entirely over this horrific event. Lenette and I were still in shock, although relieved and elated with the realization that Heidi saved Brutus and us from injury, or worse.

The campers and staff had been at camp for about a week when I told them the entire story one evening at campfire. I concluded with a warning to be careful if they came across the husky. I knew the dog offered little danger to people but was a potential killer of other dogs.

In the first few years of camp, several campers and staff had brought their pets with them. This proved to be good for the kids, and few problems resulted. While most of the visiting pets stayed at camp, Heidi spent almost all her time down at the corral with Kim, a fabulous horse wrangler. Amazingly, she kept the horses under strict control when kids were at the corral.

Sometime later, we were at the neighbor's lake for swim safety lessons. During lessons and fun, one camper yelled the husky was off-leash. A staff member had their dog with them, and the husky was heading for it. I quickly snatched up the dog and headed out to the end of the diving board. But the campers remembered the story I told them at campfire and began to scream for Heidi.

When she heard the call of the campers, she leaped into action, crossing the field in seconds. When the husky saw her coming, he turned and ran for his life, heading for his barn and safety. Still, he couldn't outrun Heidi. She struck powerfully, knocking him to the ground, where he flipped onto his back and surrendered immediately. Heidi stood above him for a long moment before turning towards the campers and returning for a hero's welcome. None that shared this experience will ever forget it.

Heidi, Brutus, And Cleo

11 October 2021

When Heidi joined our family as a puppy, Brutus took on the role of mentor to her. And Heidi, who ultimately grew into a massive German shepherd, came to adore her little friend. In fact, they were twins in how they cooperated and communicated. Here's an example: We bought a steak for dinner, which for us was a rare purchase. Lenette placed the steak carefully on the BBQ and left it for only a few moments.

Heidi and Brutus both knew that what we set on the BBQ was for us, and they would get whatever scraps were left over.

Brutus was with Lenette the entire time she was preparing our elegant meal while I prepared the BBQ. Heidi and Cleo were off playing with Cleo's kittens, a very backyard family scene. In this tranquil setting, Brutus was calculating the height of the BBQ and where the steak would be placed. This was going to be a job for Heidi.

Lenette placed the steak on the grill, and we both went inside. I to finish preparing the salad, and Lenette to prepare the balance of the banquet. Brutus went to get Heidi, who easily grabbed the steak off the grill and dropped it onto the grass where Cleo, Brutus, and she enjoyed a fabulous steak dinner.

We always shared food with them, so we never had experienced a prior "theft." But it happened. Guilt may have oozed out of them, but it didn't stop them from enjoying the steak. And so it goes with animals you love.

On another day in the '50s, Lenette was planting flowers on the front lawn. Brutus, our brilliant beagle, was relaxing with her when a German shepherd from down the street attacked him. The attack was entirely unprovoked, but we knew the dog and were aware of its aggressive behavior with other dogs. The dog's owners had already paid hefty fines for its past attacks. As a result, the animal was always supposed to be leashed and under control. Yet, on this occasion, he wasn't.

Heidi was in the backyard and, on hearing the commotion, leaped our six-foot fence to defend Brutus. This is not what the attacking dog wanted. He feared Heidi and usually avoided our house when running free. But there is more. Cleo, our very productive kitten producer, cleared the fence right behind Heidi and joined the battle. It was not pretty. While Heidi was ferociously tearing into the aggressive dog, it got worse for him when Cleo flew onto his head and began ripping at his eyes.

I quickly got our animals off the dog, but the damage was done. The fight left the attacker in bad shape, and the defeated bully retreated home, where his owners were forced to put him to sleep that day. Our three animals returned to the backyard, acting as if nothing untoward had occurred. Brutus suffered some minor bleeding, but otherwise was fine.

Beginning in 1960, each spring we would move a whole bunch of stuff to Camp Shasta to prepare for staff and campers before they arrived at camp. No 600-mile trip could be wasted, so we moved as many items as possible. A typical trip might include a water ski boat, kayaks, sailboat, and on one of the first trips, a filly, the kids at Purple Sage named "Sy-The-Clown." Eventually, we shortened her name to "Cyclone."

Cyclone, the filly, grew up with Heidi, Brutus, and Cleo and honestly thought she was one of the family. And they treated her as if she was. On the trip up to camp with all of our animals, we would stop for breaks. When we did, we all went for a walk, usually at night. People stopped whatever they were doing to witness our unlikely parade. We must have looked like a page out of the story of Noah's Ark!

ON AGING—A PERSONAL JOURNEY

On Aging—My View
01 September 2016

A friend asked if I'd write about aging. I'll give it a try. Since I'm not too far from entering the nineties (in three-plus months), I ought to be able to write or say something about growing older. I do not speak for others and will do my best to share what I know or believe to be true. What follows are my present experiences.

I recognize that aging is a complex subject and that I am going through phases or periods of being what I was, being what I am, and even thinking about what I might be. Clearly, it is not easy to "broad brush" aging, other than acknowledging it is something I'm working hard to understand. I just as soon as not think about it, but I find this to be impossible.

First and relative to my past, I still feel capable of teaching about power and its offshoots, such as relationships, communication, and leadership. In fact, I often find myself thinking about these subjects and their importance in all of our lives. I also sense that I understand the issues with greater clarity than previously. Why? Because I have more time to think about my many experiences.

Previously, everything was about preparation and execution. Digging for significant insights and understanding was my first task, followed by sharing in the most enlightened way possible. My intentions were to be pragmatic instead of philosophical, and now I feel I am more philosophical. I've come to believe philosophy is the earth that gives life to what is pragmatic.

Looking back, I know how the past-present and the past-future fully occupied my time and energy. Although I did not control the events of that time, I thought I could, and even if it was impossible, I still tried. Amid everything we created and were responsible for, Lenette and I found time and ways to explore the physical world and its people. Somehow, it all worked out well.

The second part of what I am experiencing is my being present and in the moment. Everything, each day, offers something special and enjoyable for me. Sharing time with Lenette has always been my first choice. Today it is even more so. Also, every minute I spend looking at trees, flowers, birds, the river, sky, and colors gives me pleasure. As do the people I am blessed to share time and dialogue with. Even composing this brief essay is a joy and a challenge for me.

In all things, I don't anticipate completion and, in fact, do not set a time to do so. Instead, I'm allowing myself to be in the middle of whatever I am doing and letting it unfold in its own particular way.

A brief pleasantry to share: On the way to the gym, where I work out five days a week, is an eagle's nest. For the last six or seven years, two eagles arrive, settle in on their large nest high in the tree, lay eggs, and soon care for three to four eaglets. Almost daily, Lenette and I drive by the tree and nest to view the eagles. We feel blessed to witness their family life until they all depart before summer. And yes, we look forward to next spring and the eagle's return.

The third part of my triad is the future. What the future holds is a mystery that unfolds each moment as we move into it, always aware of its unpredictability.

Life a special gift
I know this and am grateful
Events dictated

Live And Love Now

18 September 2016

Those who requested my thoughts on aging have opened a can of worms. Interestingly, my recent papers on aging have produced a significant response. Having always given effort to being there for those I worked with and served, it's evident that this is a hot subject and calls out for me to say more.

To begin, I certainly believe each of us approaches aging in our own unique way. Some fear it and do whatever they and their money can to overcome those fears. They may try, but to what avail? Time is limited for all. I live each day as best I can and recommend that all do the same. Now is good enough; be grateful and loving to yourself and others.

My primary anchor to life and living is Lenette, followed by an exercise routine and a proper diet. Also essential are our friends. How blessed Lenette and I are to have many. Other additions to this list are reading and creative writing, which force me to think. Also, the ancient adage has become my mantra: Be as fully here and now as possible. That was something I had trouble with when I was younger. It was always one foot in the present and one foot in the future. Today, it's all about living and loving now.

I will continue to write and speak about aging and share my thoughts on the subject. A reminder: this is about me, and if it offers a bit of a road map for you, maybe that's a good thing. Finally, (the proper word here) I do not waste my time pondering longevity. The future is not mine to know, so I let it be. Today is my gift, and I do my best to love my way through it.

Life's the gift to live
Waste not what is so precious
It is here and now

What's Important
08 July 2019

More than any other reason, my wife Lenette is why I'm here. I believe that a relationship with someone special is of immense importance to longevity. I want to be with her as long as possible, but understanding that I won't be a burden to her. If the time comes when I am, I'll be ready to let life go.

With Lenette being essential to my desire to remain around as her partner, what can I do to assist my continued stay? I exercise five days a week. I read a great deal of history mixed with current events and enjoy the companionship of friends.

Lenette feeds us lots of fish, vegetables, and fruit. Breakfast is a protein drink—nuts for lunch and a delicious dinner prepared by Lenette, including a generous salad. My contribution is doing the dishes.

My routine at the gym consists of two hours of exercise on Monday, Wednesday, and Friday and slightly less on Tuesday and Thursday. All five days include aerobics and muscle groups, and I am slowly improving my strength. If a decline is taking place, it is hardly noticeable. Living in the present is my reality. I take each moment as a gift.

My essays are essential for me. Comments and suggestions motivate much of my writing. I also recognize that I'm more thoughtful about things than ever before. In the past, when events occurred, I gave little thought to my actions. When circumstances demanded, I reacted as best I could. Perhaps aging is that time for reflection on things past? This is true for me.

I appreciate being here and feeling as I feel. I am lucky because I'm mentally fit, am still creative, read lots, and enjoy being with Lenette. Aging is real. Don't fear it and don't run from it. Take each day as it comes and do your best to be grateful and give love.

Changes
10 November 2019

We're moving to a senior living environment not too far from where we are, but we are leaving the river, which isn't easy. We love it here, where we have been for almost twenty years. We've traveled the world, and the extraordinary beauty of this place puts it at the very top of the list. It's right on the magnificent Truckee River, across from a park, and when the trees drop all their leaves, they reveal the Sierra Mountains. We're so grateful to have lived here.

Cleaning up, boxing, throwing things out, and giving stuff away; downsizing is a challenging task. It must be done because we are moving to one-third of our current space. Of course, we take nothing with us, anyway. Our memories are what we keep, and we consider ourselves lucky to have them, both good and bad. We also realize that "things" are just that and must be gotten rid of. We are getting it done, but while necessary, it's not easy.

There will be many changes. Instead of being entirely on our own, we will have housekeepers clean our apartment weekly. Otherwise, we'll continue living our lives and fulfilling our responsibilities as we have been.

The facility offers three restaurants that serve meals, among other amenities provided in this four-story complex. There's an indoor swimming pool, exercise area, movie theatre, gardens, transportation, and more. We might compare this to resort living, where everything is provided. We will certainly find out!

The difficult decision was when to make this move. We certainly feel like we can continue living in our three-story condo, but who knows what each day will bring? It is much better for us to make these decisions when we choose rather than wait for others and events to make them for us. The die is cast. This will all take place this coming December.

Apart from this move, most things will remain as they are. My writing is important to me and will continue as long as I believe I have something to say about entrepreneurship, leadership, power, and the absolute necessity for dialogue. Our problems with each of these issues continue to grow.

Although technology is becoming a necessity in our daily lives, it does not appear to have improved our relationships. Despite the ease of use, faster communication doesn't appear to have solved many of the "pre-tech" problems in how we relate to each other.

In my efforts to make relationships work between people, dialogue and understanding are my goals and have been for many years. I firmly believe that authentic communication is better served when we are face-to-face.

We are moving on
We know where, but not its contents
the book not yet read

Time is limited
And the river keeps flowing
Time waits for no one

The journey is short
Smell each rose and see the sky
Feel the path you walk

Our Move
25 December 2019

The move is over, but not the unpacking of boxes. This entire experience has tested us unimaginably, and Lenette and I have agreed we will do just about anything to never have to do this again! Our advice to others is to begin the down-sizing process as soon as possible. Ideally, one should have no time limit and go at it room by room. We gave much away and threw out even more. Our history now lives solely in our memory, and the rest— pictures, slides, movies, letters, etc., have been thrown away. Others wanted a few albums (remember them?), and we were thrilled to pass them on.

We have been a bonanza to charities. Name it, and we gave them boxes filled with household goods, clothes, and things they deem valuable and likely to sell. What amazed us was the number of people who shop in those stores. They were always crowded when I showed up with our SUV full of stuff for them. We hope our "things" will be turned into money for their cause. Our favorite proved to be our local animal charity.

At first, it was traumatic parting with our years of history, letters, articles, books, and items accumulated from around the world. Just the letters from staff and clients stretched beyond 12 inches in file folders. During this process, we realized the effect we had on the lives of many others. Not because we wanted to do so or be acknowledged for this, but simply by doing our job. We always did the best we could in any situation.

We always believed we had remarkable people working with us. What creative and giving people they all were. Of course, there were different degrees of talent, creativity, and attributes. We tried to nurture them all, not only because they represented us, but because of the relationships they would nurture with those they watched over, educated, and cared for.

This experience for us has been sad and challenging mostly, but we relived many good feelings and shared memories. It was impossible to avoid reviewing our history, and so we did. It helps to talk this stuff out, and we did.

Also, I need to thank the many that wanted to help us. We turned the vast majority down because we felt it essential to go through this experience as much by ourselves as possible. The few we let in to help did a magnificent job for us. In fact, we would not have gotten through this by doing it alone. Our age made it clear that regardless of our desires, help was and is necessary. Thankfully, we got it in spades!

So now, a new chapter begins for us. We will do our best to live it as well as we lived our prior chapters. As we have always known, we realize that each day is precious and that living in the present is what we must do. It's one day at a time, with the desire to live out many of them. We make this same wish for each of you to live well and with love.

Time is our present
It opens to us each day
We are so grateful

From Lynette:
As usual, Sy is the eloquent one of the family. I am so fortunate to have him in my corner. This is a time of reflection and joy for the New Year and new experience. Fond wishes to all!

Settling In
14 January 2020

We are in the adjustment period—still opening boxes and doing our best to turn 816 square feet into a comfortable living space. The apartment is actually smaller than our first home. Despite that, we made the second bedroom into the best office we've had in years, considering we operated in our cellar for the last two decades.

Our apartment is on the fourth floor on the south/west corner and has a magnificent unobstructed view of Mt. Rose and the Sierras. Our second bedroom office also has an incredible view. A big picture window lights the front room and delights us with vistas of mountains and weather. Our previous views of the Truckee River are tough to replace, but our new office setting and views greatly contribute to our feeling at home.

One of our friends set us up with a computer and related stuff. He's a miracle worker when it comes to technology. Other friends gave us physical and emotional support. We have experienced remarkable love and a willingness to be there for us. As I wrote previously, we had to turn many away from helping us. Downsizing was an experience we had mostly to face ourselves. It's not a happy one, but necessary for every human at some point in their lives. As Kurt Vonnegut wrote at the end of chapters in *Slaughterhouse-Five*, "And so it goes."

So we are moved, most boxes opened, and contents used, given away, or thrown away. Our memories we have kept. They are well established in our minds and hearts. While many "things" are gone, our memories remain strong and will stay with us. Now it's time to make ourselves as much at home as possible.

It's important to put the past aside and make the present the essential part of our lives. We can do that because we have done it many times before. Working with people, creating, building, and moving into the future once we have established ourselves in the present has been our way.

Change will occur, and we will meet its challenges as we have in the past. Life experiences have made us what we became and who we are. That will remain the same.

All of this is a novel experience for us in so many ways. It will push us to adapt, and we will if it is to our liking. And if not, we will make changes as we always have and always will.

Today, a new day
Who knows what it brings? No one!
We play the hand dealt

Let yesterday go
The river of life takes it
Not to be again

Our New Reality
19 March 2020

Some general information about our new home: This is a fifty-five-year-plus living environment. There are a hundred and twenty-five one- and two-bedroom apartments, a workout gym, heated salt-water indoor pool, dining room, bar and lounge, meeting and game rooms, and lovely grounds. Also available is a twenty-four-hour front desk concierge and bus service as needed. Various activities are scheduled each day, but people are on their own to opt in or not. For example, with some help, Lenette and I are learning the game of bridge. We're finding it to be a great game and play frequently.

Breakfast, lunch, and dinner are served, and residents pay each month for a set number of points deducted based on the meals they eat. Lenette and I have breakfast and lunch in our apartment. We make it a point to have dinner in the dining room so we can get to know most of the other residents. Those we've met and have spent time with are enjoyable and interesting individuals. We are developing into a caring group, and our being there for each other is clearly taking place.

Having built a number of communities, Lenette and I are intimately aware of the many difficulties common to staffing, training, organizing, and operating a facility to turn it into a community to benefit others. The challenge is to make what is built and staffed into the best environment possible.

Whether people are educated, professional, or not, they must be respected as the individuals they are. This means that all involved contribute to what is best for everyone. By that, I mean every resident and every employee.

I live here and now
Tomorrow is its own day
Promises wasted

We Are Learning
12 April 2020

The changes Lenette and I are going through include learning more about the technology we've tended to avoid in the past. Using an iPad is one example, and fuller use of our computer is another. The ongoing pandemic makes the need for communication without being face-to-face a necessity in our daily lives. Living in the senior complex gave us the new experience of meeting people our age. That had never happened before, since our world always had to do with youth, young professionals, and entrepreneurs.

Since we have no desire to diminish our ability to communicate, we have needed to make better use of technology. We are doing this but still look forward to the old-fashioned way of being together and enjoying each other face-to-face.

Technologies of almost every kind are the younger generation's necessity. Cell phones and other devices are attached to them in ways far beyond the tools most of us seniors consider essential. But now, seniors have increasingly adopted technology to stay connected with family and friends. Also, devices easily carried in a back pocket have replaced family picture albums and scrapbooks. Clearly, the differences between generations are increasing!

Each moment means what?
It means opportunity
It is lost or used

94th Birthday
10 December 2020

I want to thank everyone who called or sent me a birthday card. I feel so fortunate. Thank you all for remembering my birthday (5 December 1926). Here's a bit more about why I believe I am what I am.

My parents were and will always remain my role models. My mother gave love unconditionally, and my father never set limitations on any of his family. They and my five brothers and sister are gone.

Pete was my oldest brother, followed by Annette (our only and most wonderful sister), then by Hy, Joe, me, and Bob. We grew up during the "great depression" in mostly 3rd-floor apartments with a single bathroom. The first time I actually had my own bed was in the Army.

Pete was almost blind and could not enlist in the army as hard as he tried. He made torpedoes during the war. Hy enlisted right after Dec. 7th. They stationed him in New Guinea, where he was wounded and spent many months recovering in military hospitals. Joe was part of the Invasion of Normandy and the Battle of the Bulge. I spent the war on Okinawa, and Bob was a medic in Korea. I am an amalgam of them all.

One of the most beautiful stories I remember happened after staff and children had left Camp Shasta. My father, who spent the entire summer there (this was his last summer at camp), came up to Lenette and me and placed his arms around the two of us. We were giving camp a final touch-up cleaning before we left for LA.

He said, "When you graduated from UCLA, it disappointed me that you did not become a psychologist. But witnessing what the two of you do for others at camp, I realized that the work you both do is a wonderful gift you give to them all. I am so proud of you both."

This came from my father, a laborer and a carpenter with no formal education. Yet, he taught so many the art of the hammer and saw. What a man!

Here I am, celebrating my birthday. Looking back, I am grateful for my family, friends, and the love of my life, Lenette. I knew I loved her from the moment I interviewed her for a job at Purple Sage. Nothing has changed since those moments, except now I'm ninety-four.

Life is so unknown
We live each day and know this
Enjoy the moment

Time is given me
I choose to waste none of it
So I swing the bat

I strike out often
So what, if I do my best
A lesson to learn

Life is so fragile
We know this for what it means
Therefore play a part

The Benefits Of Community

21 March 2021

There are benefits to living in a community where social interaction is a daily occurrence. Each evening, we go to dinner and enjoy a meal with other residents. Either we are invited to join two other people, or we invite two people to join us. At the dinner table, we enjoy a wonderful few hours of conversation and the sharing of histories. Everyone has a story to tell, so sharing a table makes the telling of tales possible.

The beauty of this is that we get to know each other. Our histories, what we did for a living, where we grew up, and bits about family. It is an enlightening experience to be with people who have lived and continue to live interesting lives. Of course, this is not always the case, but the chance to meet fascinating people is there, and dining together is an easy way for this to happen.

Some residents remain apart from social opportunities. They may have family living within the area and spend most of their time with them. Their lives are lived apart from other residents, which is their loss. Although family and friends are especially important, the chance to make new friends at the trail's end is no small thing. All of us need relationships beyond family and old friends if we are to continue to grow instead of just getting old.

Growing old is an attitude as well as a fact. As far as the aging process goes, there is little to talk about. However, there is much to be said about the attitude. That subject is worthy of books upon books and much discussion. Aging is a condition none can avoid, so those who are old and give in to waiting for their last breath can only be pitied. Those who continue to mix with others and live as fully as possible are wise and thrive. Life should not be wasted, whether limited by old age or other factors. The opportunity to learn and give back is restricted only by our own behavior.

An excellent example is what took place at dinner a few nights ago. We joined a lovely lady we knew and a gentleman we had not met before. It turned out to be an evening full of stimulating dialogue between us. Our conversation took us to the problems which divide our country today. The gentleman led the conversation, and his knowledge of the subjects we discussed was impressive. For two hours, we engaged, and time flew by. We can hardly wait to do this again. Need I express the importance of this?

Life offers so much
Pay attention and receive
To learn is a gift

More Thoughts On Aging

01 September 2021

Again, I'm compelled to write about my aging process. Maybe there's a lesson for some others, or maybe not, but this is about me. I consider myself lucky. This coming December 5th I will be ninety-five years young. I'm feeling fine; I still exercise, read, write, enjoy being with people, and am very aware that time is precious.

I have a sense of three very distinct parts of my life. The first is the now. It is where I live, spend much of my time, and try to be with every minute of the present. That means listening as best I can to what others are saying. This is difficult since I wear earpieces, and the sounds in our dining room bounce off walls and resonate throughout the large room. I concentrate on what is said, not what I have to say. This is fine with me since I've spent much of my life getting people to listen to me. As a result, I'm learning lots more about others and worrying less about what they learn from me.

Another important part of my life is my history. I do not live in my history, but I use it to explain the reasons behind my attitude and behavior toward things in the present. I draw from my history and do my best to clarify that it is a resource I access and never confuse it with current events. Also, I consider myself fortunate to have excellent recall, and I use this in my storytelling.

Finally, the day will come that is our final day. We all have a diminishing future. It is important to maximize each moment, and I do. Whether with Lenette, friends, my cat, Mia, or enjoying our snuggly bed, I fear not and know I've been blessed. So have most of us.

Please don't interpret this as a premonition of anything. I feel I'll be around for a good couple of years. I'm still enjoying—so why not?

Diminishing Choices
11 December 2021

Now that I'm ninety-five, I'm determined to stay active with my mind. I'd like to do this with my body, but it's not the same. For someone who has been physically active most of their life, I am having some difficulty with my oxygen. I guess that's the way it is.

Regardless, I will do my best to stay creative and write every now and then. Your thoughts and comments influence me on what ends up being posted on my blog. I often write in response to requests I've received. Keep reaching out with your ideas, and I'll do my best to get them on paper.

As for my being and getting older, I have this to say. As we age, things happen to us that take our choices away. My being short of breath is not a choice, but a fact. So I take action in the evenings. With oxygen, I can enjoy a good night's sleep. So far, I have done well during the day without needing it.

Lenette is my blessing. She watches over me and makes sure that everything I do helps me get better. It's what she does, and it's working. Obviously, she's my best medicine.

I am me; who else?
And glad I am that person
Have never wanted else

Why want to be else?
I am what I am and been
Enough just being

Pure Love
11 March 2022

Death is not my problem. I'm prepared for that eventuality and have been for many years. I knew that growing up on the streets of Chicago, where I developed a reputation for being a fighter that carried across ghetto lines.

But the story is not about me, but about Lenette. What I'm about to describe happened about four weeks ago, and its effect on me continues. Before then, Lenette was becoming progressively forgetful and confused. Yet, on that day, she was so worried about me she set aside all other things and issues.

Lenette's concern was so consuming that I realized then that she needed me as much as I needed her. Amazingly, at the moment I decided I must stay alive for now and care for her, her confusion disappeared! From then on, I started getting better in every possible way, and so did she. In all aspects, Lenette began to be fully and completely herself.

The power of love is that important. Witnessing her helplessness with the time and effort she gave me was too much to bear. I realized I needed to live for her so she could live for herself.

So, not only did I get better, but Lenette has become more vital and present. A miracle, for sure, but not surprising, considering love is such an essential part of our relationship. We are so much more because of each other. She and I will do our best to keep this wellness going between us. How blessed we are!

We love and love back
We grow because of this love
How blessed we are

More On Aging
17 April 2022

I will share with you what it's like going on toward ninety-six. One must be there to know, and I'm there. Anyone younger who believes they understand aging is fooling themselves. Perhaps what I share will help you understand your aging parents better. I certainly hope so.

First, my body is wasting away, and any exercise seems futile. I weigh much less, but I also eat much less. I'm shrinking before my eyes. At eighteen, I was 5 feet, 9 inches, and weighed 180. Today I am 5 feet 6 inches and weigh about 130. For exercise, I can enjoy relatively long walks if the weather is warm enough for my liking.

Walks are special for me because I could not go five feet four months ago without stopping to catch my breath. I used oxygen twenty-four hours a day. Today, I am off oxygen and can walk long distances with no shortness of breath. Is this normal? Not according to my hospice nurse. She says I'm the rarest bird she has worked with. Oh well, that's aging for me.

My mind remains sharp. Essays, poetry, and Haiku pour out of me. I remain creative and enjoy genuine dialogue with the many wonderful people who visit and bring goodies.

Clearly, aging is unique to all those experiencing it. I'm old and grateful to be here as I am. I enjoy each day as a gift and accept what lies ahead. Whatever will be, will be. I'm okay with that.

Old is different
Each person that gets there knows
It is what it is

Life is an unknown
So let it come as it will
Today is our day

Another Way Of Looking At Aging
21 May 2022

It should be clear that my aging is a non-problem. I'm thrilled to be my age, and each day is its own with no concern for the morrow. If I make it to tomorrow, that's a good thing, but this day is my blessing, so I live it as best I can. But this is me.

Some aging people live in a state of frustration because they are unable, or have great difficulty, to do today what they could do yesterday. Being able and then suddenly unable is painful, both emotionally and mentally. Yet, getting older is unavoidable.

All of us had to live our life as it came to us. Some were more successful and achieving than others, but live our lives we did. As we did, successes and failures came our way. Whether we enjoyed and grew from them, or if they merely came and went leaving little or no impact on us, is critical. Look back on your experiences, and they tell the story.

The story also is about our relationships. My history was full of people, and I know, without question, that their influence changed me and added much to who I was constantly becoming. As I've written, my Japanese prisoners taught me much about communication and relationships. We cared for each other as a family, and we were.

I also mentioned that the captain of our company on Okinawa influenced the rest of my life. He made me understand I was capable of much more than I believed before our brief interaction. To this day, those experiences still resonate within me.

Some who are aging may have placed too much on what they were. Their expectation that the past will continue to be is a false road to follow. My wish for them is that they would look down at the steps they are taking from now on instead of looking backward at what was. I see the path before me and look forward to those unknown horizons.

What Visiting Means To Us

13 June 2022

We are not unique when it comes to being with friends and family. We love and enjoy every minute of our time together. While we never know what our conversation will be about, it's always an excellent dialogue because we are there for each other and fully present. It's the best.

We relish the gift that each visitor is to us. They often bring memories, and we share them with gusto, laughing and sometimes shedding tears full of gratitude. But sharing brings to the present some happenings in the past that we never knew of.

As guardians, Lenette and I embraced our responsibilities. Still, youth, being what it is (and ought to be), had their own ideas. We hear their stories now and love to listen to them. They broke a few rules and crossed even more lines. Youth needs to be youth, and of course, they were. As adults, they all turned out to be our kind of people.

The beauty of these visits is twofold. We relive amazing stories from our past together and have serious discussions about the present. Still, how can these conversations not be serious? Our visitors do not worry about themselves but about their children, grandchildren, and great-grandchildren. Nothing about our world is as it was. So while reliving the past is a good thing, none of our visitors live only in their history. We experience them as being fully aware of the problems that our nation and world face.

We share frank dialogues now as we did so often in the past. Being able to experience this is something we all hold on to and value. Most people do not have this good fortune, but we do and cherish every moment we are together.

I am what I am
I do not need or want more
All is what it is

Time Flies
(04 July 2022)

How often do we wait to do many things? Like calling or visiting loved ones or friends? Or reading a book we've wanted to read? What about having dinner at the restaurant everyone is raving about?

As we grow older, we appreciate all the experiences we've had. Yet, we also know that with everything we've done, we could have and should have done more. It's never about money or time. It's only about pushing the button and going for it.

Lenette and I would have missed much if we had waited to do things only because of money. We never had big money, not because we did not make a good living, but because we used our dollars for the needs of our programs and people. Those were our choices, and we lived by them. Yet, we paid our bills when they came due and still traveled and explored the world, regardless.

We bought a pop-top VW in Germany, traveled, and camped throughout most of Europe. "Donka," our VW, took us on a seven-and-a-half-month adventure through Mexico that turned into a memorable experience that was mystical and spiritual.

What if we did not do this but waited or decided to not go? An important part of our life would have never been lived. Sadly, we eventually sold our VW for what we bought it for. We all make mistakes, and looking back, that was one of them.

So, don't wait. Life and time continue to expire, but our memories remain. Make as many as you can.

We live only now
Waiting may not be too wise
Here and now is all

193

Aging Differently?
11 August 2022

Is it possible that men and women age differently? Are there significant differences between us that ought to be seriously researched? Specifically, I mean: Do females react differently than males to the problems of aging?

I am part of a population ranging from the late seventies to ninety-plus. For nearly the last several years, we have lived in a Senior Village, where most residents are single women, mainly from the East Coast. They moved to Reno because their adult children and grandchildren live and work here. Proximity to their caregivers and families becomes a necessity.

I have learned through conversation and observation that men appear to live more in the present and take each day as it comes. Yet, and this is admittedly pure speculation on my part, it seems that women are not happy losing their former selves. Giving up the past and who we have been is never easy for anyone who has lived a reasonably good life. This I can understand.

As a former teacher, creator, student of power, and problem solver, I now write these essays to make up for the activities and challenges that once flooded my existence, but are no more. Regardless, I consider each day a gift that may or may not come again.

Aging is a fact
We need to accept this fact
Let be what we are

How I'm Aging
09 July 2022

I am aging, as we all are, but I'll wager our differences are considerable. You are going to be (fill in the blank)? And I am going to be ninety-six. Who would have thunk? I intend this essay to share more of what I am going through up to and including this moment. What will be tomorrow is not my concern. No one escapes aging. Even a baby begins the process at conception.

I feel good and go for daily walks. I also try to write about a subject that Lenette and I have recently discussed. Usually, it's topics and issues that occurred in the last day or two. We remain connected to the events taking place in our country and the world. There's much to comment on and not a thing we can do anything about!

For many years, I've had dry macular degeneration. The process is slow and insidious; until recently, it never proved to be a problem. I can see well enough without glasses, but reading is becoming more difficult. With glasses, I can still work at the computer. Software allows me to increase letter size and enlarge what I must read. When necessary, I'll resort to a magnifying glass.

That aside, the good news is hospice has cut me from their program. I'm too healthy for them at this point, but they will take me back when we need their help. While I feel good about that, I will miss my visiting nurses. They have been wonderful and have become part of our family. This is how I am aging—my love for Lenette is why.

Live each day, enjoy
This day is what counts the most
Only now a gift

Old Friends
15 August 2022

Nothing is better than when we engage with old friends. Conversations range from today's news to our first coming together. Whether family, childhood friends, campers, staff, or the many I've worked with over the years, it's fun to share old stories, and we have lots of them!

As we age, all the people I've mentioned help us live each day fully. Memories are the best when they bring back an abundant past. Revisiting the good times is fun for everyone when we come together. Any sour history is best left undisturbed.

What is surprising is how we can recall and even picture those special moments. Equally gratifying is how past relationships have become today's vital conversation. There is nothing like being face to face where we are all entirely present with each other. There is no better place to be than together and in the same here and now.

This is not just about Lenette and me; togetherness is a joy shared by all humans. People need people, beginning at birth and continuing to their last moments. We would hope that this happens with everyone, but not all are lucky enough to have this experience. Nearly everywhere, the streets are filled with the mentally ill, the lost, poor, and helpless people who do not, and perhaps cannot, experience what it means to be one with others.

Engaging with family, friends, and even the people we meet today is essential for the well-being of all.

People need people
Barbra sings this so so well
It is a pure truth

Aging—A New Mindset

31 August 2022

As usual, I offer the following as my opinion and not a fact. What I share is based on my observations over these last three years.

For most people, and perhaps for all, aging is a process where it becomes apparent they are not the person they were. Not long ago, most were caregivers. They earned a living and cared for their family. What mattered was that they felt productive and their lives had purpose. They were needed—not in need.

As this mindset disappears, new feelings emerge. They may include anger, sadness, emptiness, and for a few, a sense of relief that their daily battle to survive is over. Regardless, we are not who and what we were, and suddenly, or not so suddenly, our role and way of life are no more.

These points are not to be dismissed. Getting old is closing one's life and writing the last chapter of a one-of-a-kind and extraordinary book. When people have lived full and challenging lives, most are fully aware that "the fat lady" is close to finishing her song. Even for those in denial, this truth cannot be long ignored. How long the candle will still burn is not in our hands. All we can hope for is that it's a long-lasting wick.

We are born and live
What comes our way we can't know
It is our life lived

Communicating With The Aging

02 September 2022

I speak only for myself; others may view their aging process as something they have earned. Some consider it a just reward for having lived a productive life. Still, there are those who cry and long for what is no more and, worse, what can never be again. Also, some absolutely fear death and the nothingness that awaits them.

None of this frightens me any more than the typhoon and the giant waves I faced on the way to Okinawa. I did not fear then, and I do not fear now. Events dictate—not us.

Here are a few words on communicating with an aging person who is important to you. Be as present with them as possible. Listen, I mean seriously listen, and be patient. Don't mistake their ability to find the right words for senility. Tell them what you heard being said and what you understood. Don't play-act to make them feel good. They will see through any sugarcoating or condescension. Be who you really are and acknowledge what you feel. When you are given the time and space to respond, do so and be candid.

When I visited my father after his stroke, he made a cutting motion across his throat with his hand. He was ready to die, and I made sure he saw my eyes, showing that I understood and approved his plea. He passed soon after I gave him my support. Isn't that what love means? Those we love deserve nothing less.

Aging—Not For the Weak
10 September 2022

Lenette and I appear to be lucky ones. What else can explain our physical, mental, and emotional state? Living in a senior environment and witnessing a population of older people is an entirely new experience for us. Over the years we have lived here, the changes we've seen in ourselves and others have become more evident.

One day our friends and acquaintances are walking upright, and then, the next time we see them, they are relying on aids such as canes and wheelchairs. We see or hear of one or two being taken to the hospital, living on oxygen, or simply looking older than the day before. Others we never see again. These are the unavoidable day-to-day realities in our senior environment.

The end will come to us in time. We do not know when, nor do we worry about it. And we do not give in to what we realize is inevitable. We will get there soon enough. This does not overly concern us or interfere with our continuing to live as best we can. We let each day unfold as we read, write, exercise, and enjoy meals with good friends.

We live in the present. The past exists as a file of memories to visit now and then, but we do not live there or in the future. More and more, it is just day-to-day. But there are special times too, and that is when we have visitors who share our history.

It is marvelous to be with people we consider family, and it's wonderful that we have so many! It's also remarkable what we learn about our past from those we shared it with. We hear of events we were part of but did not know what was unfolding at the time. New perspectives never grow old.

A Now Thing
5 October 2022

I am about to be ninety-six. In our senior living environment, there are about 150 others within the same striking distance. As I've mentioned, where we live is not a facility where care is on site. If help at any level is needed, 911 is called.

My point here is that what we witness all around us, such as feeling well, enjoying conversation or a meal, is, at best, a now thing. Tomorrow may bring fatigue, pain, a hospital trip, or that we are no more. The path we are walking is not endless, nor is it a long one. An end is our only future.

Here are the musts for those of us on this journey. Be present and engage with people. Listen and make sure you hear them, and they hear you. Let your past be your past unless family and old friends bring it into the conversation. If experiences were pleasant, reminisce; if not, let them go.

Now is what is. Be with it and be grateful for the good things in your life and release, at last, the things that are not. We are all on the same journey, and none of us needs to walk this path alone.

A Blessing?
10 October 2022

I note that it's the people in their fifties, sixties, and seventies who do most of the writing and commenting about being old. Some claim that aging is a blessing; however, not being there and having age as their own experience makes knowing impossible.

Old means not being who you were in so many ways that I won't take the time or space to note them. There's very little about being old that might be considered a blessing, despite being fantasized as such by those not there yet.

Perhaps those younger individuals are whistling in the dark out of sheer fear of what is to come. The old do not need to conjecture. They are in the very center of the storm and have a genuine sense of its outcome. The old may not speak about this, but they know what being old is. Words themselves are inadequate.

I loved my life and the many challenges Lenette and I faced almost daily. My love for her is stronger today than ever before. I know it will all end in the not-too-distant future. So, how in the world would I take this as a blessing?

The sand not endless
It runs out on all of us
Time is limited

OTHER THOUGHTS

It's Simple
28 April 2020

We live on a relatively small planet with limited resources, and we know environmental problems are only growing. Yet, we remain in conflict and competition instead of cooperating to improve a worsening situation.

Dinosaurs lived for millions of years, but they and much of the Earth were destroyed in a mere moment. Disaster can strike from out of nowhere again, and humanity is powerless to prevent it. We see this nearly every day when some event, be it fire, earthquake, or hurricane, occurs. And now that the covid virus has emerged, it is more apparent than ever how fragile we are when dealing with nature.

There is a world of difference between us and the dynamic physical world surrounding us that controls our collective destinies. Here there is no conscience, no thought, only events that happen, and we humans suffer or benefit.

Humanity lives in the moment. It is that simple a truth. Yesterday is gone, and tomorrow has yet to come. While we know our history, one can only hope we've learned from those many experiences.

Time irrelevant
Now is all we really have
Enjoy the moment

Love each other now
Saving for tomorrow, why?
All we have is now

Truth
17 June 2020

What is truth? I find many answers to that question in religion, philosophy, and history. Ask people, and they will have their own definitions and truths. Most people firmly believe what they believe is truth, and arguing with them about what they believe usually hardens their position and alienates them from further discussion. In the worst case, relationships may suffer. The wise know that challenging another's belief invites trouble.

Are there universal truths? Although some may disagree, examples abound. Scientific evidence has shown that water entirely covered the Earth in the distant past. Today, that reality is difficult to grasp when we see mountains that reach 29,000 feet and beyond. It is equally difficult to acknowledge that giant dinosaurs once populated the planet until an asteroid wiped them out. Even more controversial is the scientific evidence which traces our heritage back to a place in Africa where human life began.

There is hard evidence that at the very beginning, we have descended from one set of parents and are all related. Over time, as our predecessors increased, they, of necessity, moved in every direction seeking food, water, and some degree of safety. Humanity had to band together in tribes because numbers meant increased safety. This led some to diverge from hunters to farmers and loose bands to form communities.

As humans migrated to every corner of the Earth, they also changed appearances—skin color, facial features, and even size and weight. Different environments made for different-looking people, but not the blood that flows within each and the brain and emotions that rule human behavior. Tribes, communities, villages, and countries emerged as humanity evolved. Yet, throughout, all forms of leadership and governance existed.

The unwillingness to accept the truth of our common origins is at the core of problems between people and nations. The refusal to accept differences has created beliefs that have justified wars and genocide. Unfathomable when one considers we are all brothers and sisters from our shared beginnings.

Still, people confuse beliefs with irrefutable truths. These exist in one's religion, economics, politics, and forms of governance. Often, belief is far more potent than the truth. Why else would some who deny truth be willing to die for their beliefs?

Be different, please
Be you and support me too
We are related

Are we different?
Yes and no and a good thing
difference a gift

My blood has a past
Roots somewhere in Africa
We are family

Focusing On The Future
06 May 2022

I used to be in two places at the same time. While I was always in the present with staff and kids, I looked to the future when the time presented itself. I was exploring the possibilities of visiting Europe as a place to hike and bike with campers and their parents. I considered including parents because many of them saw the benefits of camp. So, we discussed what they envisioned and their own needs as adults. It allowed me to look into a potential activity that was not common at the time. We also considered whether the trips would remain combined or separate, one for children and one for adults. Education and adventure were the obvious benefits.

I bring this up because focusing on the future was not an uncommon occurrence for me when time allowed. And now, I have the time to ponder the future of our world. From my perspective, the world is experiencing critical environmental difficulties, forcing changes that must be dealt with sooner rather than later. Air quality, drinking water, and growing the world's food are only a few of the mounting challenges.

If this wasn't concerning enough, consider the capabilities that many nations have to destroy it all. Based on what is happening now, the possibility of no future at all presents itself. Before there is no time left to consider what may lie ahead, we must undertake different and better ways to govern and live as the one world we are.

The nations that think they can act, live, and prosper independently are sorely mistaken. They need each other. We need to trade and exchange what is full within our basket for what is full in the others. We need to see our world as a gift none of us can do without, and we all need to share in its care.

Our Changing Planet

19 May 2022

Time is not ours to manipulate; it moves endlessly. We have no choice but to ride along and do our best to be as comfortable as possible with it.

Living on Earth is our good fortune. It is our home and provides us with amazing beauty through nature. It also provides us with an abundance of what is necessary for life. There is a sun that warms us, soil that grows our food, water to sustain all, and an extraordinary array of ways to procreate. How blessed we are.

But change is inevitable, and our Earth is changing. If we are to survive, we must change with it. It's not like we have a choice. Our options are few compared with Earth's powerful manifestations and what they demand from us.

Wholesale natural events have existed since our planet's beginnings. In fact, Earth's creation was likely the result of forces beyond imagining. So how can we remain as we are, doing little or nothing to help our world survive? There are, of course, a considerable number of people who believe humanity should leave it in God's hands and a like number of those who are merely disinterested. Others think kicking the can down the road for the next generation is the answer.

Yet, the evidence speaks loud and clear. Humanity must do everything possible to cope with the reality of our changing world. If this means a form of world government because no one nation is up to the task, then that needs to happen. Just look at the madness of Russia's unprovoked wars and ask yourself, should a single country be allowed to dictate policy and change to the rest of the world?

Time is running out
Our world in deep trouble
Who will act on this?

Thoughts On A World Government
11 May 2022

I know about power, leadership, relationships, and communication between people. This has been my continuing interest, study, and work for almost eighty years. So, my views on world government are based on only what I know.

Ideally, any governing body should be comprised of people who represent how they have come to be the adults they are. They must have demonstrated a passion for representing and speaking on behalf of the many, not the narrow interests of the wealthy and the powerful. They should see the world as a precious totality to care for without regard for borders and fences.

While I can't speak to finances and other resources, clearly a governing body requires them if it is to function. Science, technology, and education need to be fully supported. Immediate action ensuring the health and safety of the world's population should be at the top of the list. Eradicating all nuclear weapons must also be considered for the world's good.

The world belongs to each of us, so we should not need gated borders. We must grant freedom to all. A free world can foster an economy that allows people to make a good living and care for their families.

My philosophy as a leader and teacher was based on caring for all and helping people learn how to care for each other. I believe that being responsible for the well-being of Earth's population is essential to the world's survival. Time is running out.

Time is not a thought
It is running out quickly
The world is ready

Where Are We Headed?

05 July 2022

The big question is: Where are our Earth and nations heading at the present time, and what will they face in the near future? I have no idea, but I am willing to guess. I, for one, believe that time is not ours to waste. At ninety-five years old, I won't and cannot.

The problem with our environment is real. Every day, breathable air and clean drinking water are negatively impacted by human behavior. Other problems include elevated temperatures, drought, population growth, and food insecurity. There are more, of course, but I'll stop here and hope that science and a cooperative world will act in concert to address these issues, which are now spiraling out of control.

The clash between Nationalism vs. Liberalism, while a growing problem, does not compare to the global problem of a disintegrating environment. Still, these governance philosophies affect the daily lives of most people who are helpless to choose the best way to govern and live for themselves, their families, and their communities.

Fundamentally, Liberalism is about each person being able to exercise equal rights under the law. Nationalism, on the other hand, conveys these rights only to a specific population instead of all.

Our planet's resources were once considered limitless. Yet, a constantly growing population is stretching Earth's resources to the limit. We must never forget that we are on this planet together and need to care for all.

The World must act
Time is not ours to let lie
Contribute to it

Who Will Lead?

12 May 2022

I feel a global governing body might become necessary if the earth is to survive rogue nations and address things such as a changing environment, economic inequality, population explosion, national border issues, and the threat of future pandemics. These challenges are as complex as they are widespread and affect us all.

I've proposed the creation of a world government. The first question that comes to mind is who would be qualified to serve on such a world governance body. As in any government, quality leadership is a must. Critical positions such as these cannot be a training ground for those not qualified. In this, I believe age and experience are of paramount importance.

I place age first only because those extra years bring experience. I have written that the experiences which have the most significant and lasting impact on us are often repeated. Furthermore, leadership selection from this group should be restricted to include only those who have demonstrated great wisdom over the years. Ideally, they, over their lifetimes, have given much to others, especially helping the many while rejecting special and narrow interests. People like these have existed throughout the ages. Every nation and religion has given birth to them.

Age and experience aside, financial success is not a qualification that should be considered. While many of the world's population might feel that those who are immensely successful, powerful, or charismatic are the most attractive candidates for a position in a world government, the best qualification must be years of growing and caring for people. Besides their wealth, are these people noteworthy leaders adept at nurturing and growing others? Do they earnestly seek growth? And are they willing and able to provide the environment for this to happen? Their history will provide the answers.

Another necessary leadership attribute is the quality of their relationships with their key people and others. All of these exemplary leaders I speak of will have an established inner circle. Outstanding leaders have achieved their position not by accident and never by what they have done alone. They bring with them people of proven talent and a similar philosophy about caring for people and personal growth. This is why I mentioned age and experience. We should evaluate any candidate over at least 25 years of working with others. During this time, they would have created several inner circles, building them to where any member in their present inner circle could effectively problem-solve and lead as required.

Thus, it is a body of outstanding people who should enter the world government structure, not just a single person. No organization functions well with one person, regardless of how unique and capable they might be. That is why I have taught leaders how to build special relationships with certain staff members who demonstrated qualities above and beyond.

I do not know when a "world government" might emerge, but I believe it remains a possibility. In the future, natural and man-made events will make this type of solution more realistic. Nations will be forced to work together or fend for themselves amid global uncertainties and an environment out of control.

This might never happen; the danger remains that we may self-destruct. Yet, simply accepting this as how the world is and functions amounts to madness. This brings us to a crossroads of philosophies.

A recent paper details both philosophies. Written by a Stanford University professor, the essay does a superb job of defining both and arguing why the liberal nations continue to grow and why the nationalistic ones will decline and disappear[1].

Of course, I agree with him, which brings me back to my argument for a world governing body to respond to the natural and unnatural events that will affect everyone on the planet. We

---

[1] foreignaffairs.com / *A Country of Their Own*—F. Fukuyama, January 2022

can only guess what the future may bring. The willingness to confront problems proactively is part of what makes an exceptional leader. Hopefully, they are among us.

Great leaders are few
A gift to be close to them
They are not a dream

Liberals Believe
In a World For All To Live
Is there Another Way?

Power exists now
As it began on our earth
Are we listening?

A Sad State Of Affairs
27 June 2022

For some 35 years, I worked seeking understanding so I could help those in power that I worked with. In the process, I learned more about myself relative to this subject. The power issue is a global problem that is poorly and rarely understood and too often abused.

I sense disaster is heading the world's way, and I believe it's not far off. It's easy to point out that the environment is in terrible shape and that issues abound with trade and economics. Then there is Russian aggression and other rogue nations, the population explosion, and rampant disease. One would think this is plenty, but what of the state of our nation?

The work we did throughout the years with children would be impossible today. I believe the ideas and philosophy I brought to the table might fall on deaf ears today. Almost all turn to technology to address their problems in day-to-day life, and dialogue, particularly genuine dialogue, is almost non-existent. The explosion of technology has resulted in a cultural shift. Most of today's youth embrace it, forgoing the societal norms we once enjoyed and took for granted. As this trend continues to grow, the future is unclear. Our tech has become far more advanced than we are as a society.

While I see technology as a significant issue, I do not believe it is entirely at fault. The media, television in general, and other "toys" have contributed to what I feel is a breakdown in society. Along with massive amounts of information, tech also exposed us to a tremendous volume of opinions and misinformation. The problem has grown exponentially, and many fear it is driving us apart as a nation. The net effect of all this is that we are becoming more isolated, even as we continue to live together.

Although we see and talk to each other, it's not enough. As I emphasize in almost every essay I write, talk is not necessarily dialogue because authentic dialogue creates and takes place on a level playing field.

A level playing field means that power must be shared or deliberately set aside so authentic communication can occur. We must be equal if we are to have genuine dialogue. As a child or subordinate, feeling this equality contributes to our growth and sense of belonging in and to our immediate society, whether family, school, friends, or coworkers.

But genuine dialogue is rare and may be disappearing. The factors I spoke of are the reason this is so. Genuine dialogue demands that things and toys must be set aside. Besides looking at each other, we need to be entirely with each other and in the same moment. As in all things, the medium is the message.

The World changes
Humans appear to do this
I don't think so

I live here with you
We need what we each can do
This is good for all

Guns
08 July 2022

As a young man, I served in the Army. This is long past, but I will never forget the experience. I write this essay about guns because I was trained to know and fire every small arm in the military arsenal during that period.

My intro to guns began in 1945 at basic training in the infantry at Fort Hood, Texas. Here is where I shot my first rifle, a Garand. As I recall, it took a clip of seven rounds. Inserting the clip required some dexterity, or you damaged a thumb. I handled it well and received my expert pin. But this was just the beginning.

After a considerable training period, the company I trained with went off for the invasion of Okinawa. I was sent to advanced training in the signal corps, and we mainly trained in night warfare. I am seriously colorblind, but reading maps at night with very little light was a gift I had. I could also identify camouflage from the real thing.

Our training was to prepare for the invasion of Tokyo Harbor. The assault became unnecessary because of the atomic bomb(s), and I believe my life was spared as a result. We were in Hiroshima and witnessed the devastation, including the dead and dying. Because of nuclear weapons, fighting large-scale wars "*mano a mano*" has become a thing of the past.

The problem here at home is a different type of mass destruction. Automatic weapons in the hands of young and troubled people. I can think of no good reason for any citizen to have or need one. We have the best trained and armed military in the world, so the defense of our country is not the issue. Hunting rifles, shotguns, and pistols meet all our personal needs for food, sports, and protection—but an automatic weapon? Come on!

The Times We Live In

09 July 2022

Covid does not back down as many other viruses have. Our tools to fight disease have never been better or more sophisticated, yet this virus continues to threaten the world's population. No person on earth is safe from contracting it, making it an issue for all. Yet, the virus is just one of many problems presenting themselves now or coming our way.

As of this writing, there is no clarity of intent between Russia and Ukraine, China and Taiwan, and the nuclear aspirations of North Korea. Climate change and political upheaval is adding to the misery plaguing Central and South America, Africa, and the Middle East.

The endangered environment and its bag of present and near-present issues are probably mere noise to many of the world's population. Taking care of day-to-day demands is already plenty to worry about. In the future, however, feeding oneself and family, finding drinkable water and breathable air will pose a problem for all humanity. Wealth will offer no protection. No one has found a way to eat or drink silver and gold.

Other challenges we face at the moment are not insignificant either. Random killings of people out in public, mass shootings of children in school, and those of different color, religion, political views, or sexual orientation have become commonplace. Consequently, those who fear future events like these might prefer isolation to the risk of placing themselves in harm's way. Where can any of the people I mention feel safe just being?

One would think and hope we have the tools to identify warped minds, particularly at early ages, where treatment is more easily done and success is more likely. This is not an unrealistic goal. While working with disturbed youth, I achieved changes in their behavior and sociability with most, if not all. I listened to them and gave them tools to deal with their anger. It is amazing what honesty and caring can do.

Selecting Leaders
02 October 2022

I've been thinking about this coming election and the issue of leadership. Two words immediately come to mind—cooperation and dialogue. How does any leader ever hope to arrive at creative problem-solving, possible consensus, or any meaningful degree of agreement without understanding these words and the importance of how they relate to each other? Please note I am only interested in sharing what I know to be true about leadership and not recommending a candidate.

Over many years, I've worked closely with young people with little or no experience in any field. If I hired them, it was because I recognized the student in them. I've always been attracted to those with potential. When I worked with experts in their chosen fields, I found they also had to accept that they were students and eager to grow. Otherwise, our working together would be wasted.

Because of my work with other entrepreneurs and professionals, I discovered leaders create the environment, not employees. And, as I've repeatedly stated, leaders are their own worst enemy. I realize there's a good reason so little of this truth has been exposed. Being a messenger is a dangerous business. Have you read Machiavelli's *The Prince* lately?

The lesson learned is that how leadership power is exerted makes all the difference in how those dependent on that power react. The environment the leader creates ripples all the way down the line and springs from their relationship and communication with those dependent on their power and influence. This is true whether the power is in the hands of a parent, teacher, businessperson, or government leader. Dialogue and cooperation must go hand in hand if there is to be growth and solutions. Keep that in mind when you choose and be sure to vote!

About the Authors

Sy Ogulnick received a BA from UCLA, a Teacher's Credential from the Los Angeles Board of Education, and completed phase I (Master's portion) in a Doctor of Behavioral Science program at California Coast University. He has created programs for children nationwide and developed successful training programs for personnel. Sy has written numerous papers on interpersonal relationships, leadership, and power. He has lectured throughout the United States and has appeared on many radio and TV talk shows.

Steve A. Zuckerman has worn many creative hats through the years. He's enjoyed a successful career in the music industry as an award winning composer, orchestrator, and producer—scoring feature films, television shows, video games, and countless commercials. His work is also featured in numerous toys and novelties. As a copywriter, he has launched many youth-centric products, like *Teenage Mutant Ninja Turtles* and *Power Rangers*, to name a few. In addition to writing novels in several of his favorite genres, Steve's creative boutique, *creativecombustion.tv* is actively engaged in producing television and internet commercials and promotions.

Other Books

ALSO BY SY OGULNICK

Leadership: Power and Consequences
Navigating Leadership, Growth and Change

ALSO BY STEVE A. ZUCKERMAN

Alien Roadkill Volumes 1-6
The Ruthless Relic
The Twisted Tomahawk
The Vindictive Vines
The Cautionary Curse
Zombiesaurs

Made in the USA
Monee, IL
06 January 2023

7a5be221-20af-4a84-8def-4f9ef7adb9adR01